90
5

D0437269

Understanding and Promoting Transformative Learning

A Guide for Educators of Adults

Second Edition

Patricia Cranton

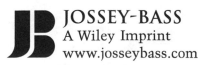

JOSSEY-BASS
A Wiley Imprint
www.josseybass.com

Published by Jossey-Bass
A Wiley Imprint
989 Market Street, San Francisco, CA 94103-1741   www.josseybass.com

Jossey-Bass books and products are available through most bookstores. To contact Jossey-Bass directly call our Customer Care Department within the U.S. at 800-956-7739, outside the U.S. at 317-572-3986, or fax 317-572-4002.

Jossey-Bass also publishes its books in a variety of electronic formats. Some content that appears in print may not be available in electronic books.

Library of Congress Cataloging-in-Publication Data

Cranton, Patricia.
  Understanding and promoting transformative learning : a guide for educators of adults / Patricia Cranton.— 2nd ed.
      p. cm. — (Jossey-Bass higher and adult education series)
    Includes bibliographical references and index.
    ISBN-13: 978-0-7879-7668-2 (cloth)
    ISBN-10: 0-7879-7668-7 (cloth)
    1. Adult learning.   2. Transfer of training.   3. Adult education.   I. Title.   II. Series.
  LC5225.L42C72 2006
  378'.196—dc22   2005036847

Printed in the United States of America
SECOND EDITION
HB Printing   10 9 8 7 6 5 4

Contents

The Jossey-Bass
Higher and Adult Education Series

Preface to the Second Edition

Interest in transformative learning has spiraled since Jack Mezirow's (1978, 1981) early works on perspective transformation and especially since the 1991 publication of his *Transformative Dimensions of Adult Learning* and my 1994 publication of *Understanding and Promoting Transformative Learning*. We gathered again, in the fall of 2005, for the Sixth International Transformative Learning conference, and we have a new journal, *Journal of Transformative Education*. Articles on transformative learning regularly appear in journals such as the *Adult Education Quarterly*, and Jossey-Bass's *New Directions for Continuing and Adult Education* series frequently includes chapters and even entire issues on the topic. Most texts devoted to providing an overview of the adult education field contain a section on transformative learning. Transformative learning is an entry in the 2005 *International Encyclopedia of Adult Education*.

Background

Historically, adult education has been seen as a political movement—a movement toward freedom and liberation that is both personal and social. During the 1970s and 1980s, theorists, writers, and practitioners tended to focus on a more humanistic approach to adult education, guided in large part by the influential writings of Malcolm

Knowles. But in the 1990s and now into the 2000s, ideology critique and social change are once again informing our field.

Transformative learning is defined as a process by which previously uncritically assimilated assumptions, beliefs, values, and perspectives are questioned and thereby become more open, permeable, and better justified. This cognitive, rational approach has been elaborated on by theorists who incorporate the role of imagination, intuition, soul, and affect into their understanding of the transformative process. Transformative learning theory has changed the direction of adult education practice.

Need

Oddly, we have few resources for practitioners. How can transformative learning be encouraged in classrooms? In the workplace? In informal self-help groups? In community development initiatives? Ed Taylor (2000a), in his analysis of the research on transformative learning theory to that date, calls for more work to be done on strategies for fostering transformative learning. He criticizes the existing publications as being "obtuse, overly academic, difficult to access, and only now and then [having] direct implications for classroom teaching" (p. 321).

If we agree, and I think many adult educators do, that transformative learning is a primary goal of adult education, we need to pay attention to how to put it into practice. Clearly, transformative learning is of increasing importance, but we have fallen behind in helping practitioners see how the theory can be relevant in their work.

I think my 1994 book, *Understanding and Promoting Transformative Learning*, has served quite well in this capacity. I am aware of it being used frequently in graduate and undergraduate courses in adult education, and I often receive e-mails from readers who remark that they find the book relevant to their practice. However, much has happened in the field in the last ten years, and this book needed to be updated.

Purpose and Audience

My 1994 book was intended to explain transformative learning theory, describe the process from the learners' perspective, explore individual differences in transformative learning, present practical strategies for fostering transformative learning, and discuss how adult educators themselves are transformative learners.

The primary purpose of the second edition remains essentially the same. I incorporate recent theoretical developments such as John Dirkx's (2000) ideas about the role of imagination and spirituality in transformation, the importance of affect in the process, Mary Belenky's (Belenky and Stanton, 2000) idea of connected knowing, and Stephen Brookfield's (2005) thoughts on critical theory. I also include my more recent work on individuation and authenticity, and my attempts to develop a holistic model of transformative learning.

Throughout the book, I focus on providing a practical and accessible approach. Since the publication of the 1994 book, I have taught courses on transformative learning at least twice a year using that book as a text. These experiences have given me a good sense of how to communicate with potential readers, and this is experience I did not have in the writing of the first edition.

The intended audiences of the 1994 book were practicing adult educators and students of adult education, faculty members and graduate students in departments of adult education, and professional developers in a variety of settings. The audience for the second edition remains the same.

As did the 1994 book, the second edition will help adult educators understand what transformative learning is, distinguish it from other forms of learning, and foster it in their practice. The first part of the book is dedicated to clarifying transformative learning theory and relating it to other theoretical frameworks. I examine transformative learning from the learner's perspective, and I discuss individual differences in how learners go through the process. In the second half of the book, the focus is squarely on strategies for promoting transformative learning in a variety of adult education contexts. Practitioners will be able to take ideas from the text and apply them directly in their teaching.

Overview of the Contents

The organization of the second edition of *Understanding and Promoting Transformative Learning* will remain the same as that of the first edition. Chapter One provides an overview of perspectives on adult learning and places transformative learning within that context. I follow Habermas's and Mezirow's categorization of instrumental, communicative, and emancipatory learning to do this. Chapter Two presents transformative learning theory. I update the theory to incorporate Mezirow's new concepts and terminology, specifically "habits of mind" and "points of view" and the addition of moral-ethical, philosophical, and aesthetic habits of mind. I describe content, process, and premise reflection in this chapter. In Chapter Three, I elaborate on Mezirow's traditional theory by reviewing the extrarational approach to understanding transformative learning, describing connected and relational learning, examining social change as a goal of transformative learning, considering transformative learning in the context of groups and organizations, and outlining the ecological view of the theory. In Chapter Four, I describe the process undergone by learners as they are engaged in transformation. In Chapter Five, I suggest that individuals experience transformative learning in different ways based on my understanding of Jung's psychological type theory.

In the second half of the book, I turn to practical strategies for adult educators who hope to foster transformative learning. In Chapter Six, I present educator roles within the framework of instrumental, communicative, and emancipatory learning. In a discussion of power, I include Foucault's conceptualization of power—an understanding of power that Brookfield has made accessible to adult educators. I also incorporate some thoughts on educator authenticity. Chapter Seven expands on the notion of empowerment; I incorporate the newer thinking about how educators and learners exercise power. The chapter provides practical strategies for empowering learners. In Chapter Eight, I include ideas for stimulating critical reflection and critical self-reflection, and I also pay attention to the intuitive and affective aspects of questioning our assumptions, beliefs, and perspectives. In Chapter Nine, I argue that the educator who fosters transformative learning has a moral responsibility to provide and arrange for support for his or her students. I suggest a number of ways in which support can be given, both within and outside of the learner group. Finally, in Chapter Ten, I discuss the adult educator's transformative journey. Included is a description, based on my research, of how educator authenticity develops with experience and how becoming more authentic is a transformative process.

Acknowledgments

I would like to acknowledge each of the adult learners with whom I have worked over the years. It is through your questioning, support, and challenges that I have developed my ideas and brought them into my practice.

I want to thank my many colleagues in the field of transformative learning whose ideas and writing have shaped my thinking. I especially appreciated the comprehensive and helpful reviews of the first draft of the manuscript provided by John Dirkx and Colleen Wiessner. And I am indebted to David Brightman and all of the good folks at Jossey-Bass who always make my work better.

It is with deep gratitude that I acknowledge the insights of Laurence Robert Cohen through both our conversations and his wide-ranging comments on the manuscript.

About the Author

Patricia Cranton received her B.Ed. degree (1971) and M.Sc. degree (1973) from the University of Calgary, and her Ph.D. degree (1976) from the University of Toronto. Patricia's primary research interests have been in the areas of teaching and learning in higher education, transformative and self-directed learning, and most recently, authenticity and individuation. She was selected as an Ontario Distinguished Scholar in 1991 in recognition of her research and writing on teaching and learning in higher education. She received the Ontario Confederation of University Faculty Association's Teaching Award in 1993 and the Lieutenant Governor's Laurel Award in 1994 for an outstanding contribution to university teaching.

Patricia Cranton's books include *Planning Instruction for Adult Learners* (1989), with a second edition in 2000; *Working with Adult Learners* (1992), also translated into Japanese in 1999; *Understanding and Promoting Transformative Learning* (1994), also translated into Chinese in 1995; *Professional Development as Transformative Learning* (1996), also translated into Japanese in 2004; *No One Way: Teaching and Learning in Higher Education* (1998); *Personal Empowerment Through Type* (1998); *Becoming an Authentic Teacher* (2001); and *Finding Our Way: A Guide for Adult Educators* (2003). Patricia has edited three New Directions volumes, *Transformative Learning in Action* (1997), *Universal Challenges in Faculty Work: Fresh Perspectives from Around the World* (1997), and

Fresh Approaches to the Evaluation of Teaching (2001), and is currently editing a fourth, *Authenticity in Teaching.*

From 1976 to 1986, Patricia Cranton was at McGill University in the Centre for Teaching and Learning and the Department of Educational Psychology and Counselling. From 1986 to 1996, she was at Brock University in the Faculty of Education. She founded Brock University's Instructional Development Office and directed it from 1991 to 1996. Patricia was Visiting Professor of Adult Education at the University of New Brunswick from 2000 to 2002 and at St. Francis Xavier University from 2002 to 2005.

Also during that time, and currently, she is adjunct professor at Teachers College, Columbia University, where she teaches courses on transformative learning both online and in a workshop format. Patricia is presently visiting professor of adult education at Penn State Harrisburg.

1

Dimensions of Adult Learning

Each time I read the introductory chapters of a graduate student's thesis, I witness the struggle to review and define adult learning. And as I look at this nearly blank screen, thinking about the many perspectives on adult learning in the literature, I wonder whether there is anything I can contribute. It is my purpose in this chapter not so much to review the different ways in which adult learning is described, but rather to create the boundaries around transformative learning theory and to situate transformative learning theory within the more general literature on adult learning. When I teach courses and facilitate workshops on transformative learning, we inevitably come to a point in our discussions where everything seems transformative. Someone will say, "But if I learn a new computer skill, that frees me to do things in a new way and I feel transformed," or another person will say, "Learning to read is a skill, but it opens up the world," and almost always, people will begin to argue that children can engage in transformative learning. When a young person rebels against her parents' rules, is that not critical reflection? It takes us some time to work our way out of these dilemmas in our conversation. We deconstruct and then reconstruct the meaning of the theory. Perhaps what I can do in this chapter is to work through some of that process and at least clarify the perspective on transformative learning on which this book is based.

Essentially, I follow Mezirow's (2000, 2003a) definition of transformative learning as a process by which previously uncritically assimilated assumptions, beliefs, values, and perspectives are questioned and thereby become more open, permeable, and better validated. However, I have been strongly influenced by the work of my colleagues who incorporate imagination, intuition, soul, and affect into their understanding of the process (Dirkx, 2001a). I no longer see transformative learning as an entirely cognitive, rational process (Cranton & Roy, 2003). This is the foundation from which I write in this book. Given that, let us return to situating transformative learning in the broader context of adult learning.

Adult Learning as a Distinctive Process

Adult learners are mature, socially responsible individuals who participate in sustained informal or formal activities that lead them to acquire new knowledge, skills, or values; elaborate on existing knowledge, skills, or values; revise their basic beliefs and assumptions; or change the way they see some aspect of themselves or the world around them. An adult learner might take classes to fulfill requirements in a Ph.D. program, participate in a training session required by her organization, learn how to ski, or join a bereavement group to understand her reactions to the death of her spouse. Learning in some form is an aspect of virtually every person's life.

Given the complexity of human differences, the diverse contexts within which people live and work, and the many types of things people learn, it seems fruitless to try to delineate general characteristics of adult learning. Yet we seem to want to be able to say that adult learning is different from children's learning, so for decades writers have tried to list those things that make adult learning distinctive. I review some of those characteristics here, though I also question how universal they are.

Adult learning is often described as *voluntary*. Individuals choose to become involved in either informal or formal learning activities because they want to develop personally, or as a response to a professional or practical need. The loss of a job, a change in lifestyle, or a move to a different geographical location may prompt someone to want to learn. When we consider adult learning as voluntary, this leads to the assumption that people are highly motivated and interested in a content that is relevant to their needs, which may or may not be true. Many people feel obligated to attend workplace learning activities, and some may be required to engage in training or retraining. For those who participate in mandated programs, a skilled facilitator or a good course can pique interest, and conversely, even when people do choose to become involved in learning, their interest may flag for a variety of reasons.

Adult learning is usually described as *self-directed*. The concept of self-directed learning has permeated adult education theory and practice to such an extent that it is almost equated with adult education. Unfortunately, the definitions of self-directed learning are varied and confusing. It was Knowles (1975, 1980) who started this when he suggested that all adults have a preference for being self-directed. The word "preference" was overlooked, and educators assumed learners were self-directed. Knowles saw self-directed learning as a process by which people made the instructional design decisions—identifying their needs, setting their own goals, choosing how to learn, gathering materials, finding resources, and judging their progress. Knowles felt that this was a distinguishing characteristic of adult learning. It was by no means intended to be an independent or isolating way of learning; however, in some of its applications it became so. Over the years, self-direction came to mean a characteristic of a person (similar to autonomy), a method of teaching, a developmental goal, and several other variations on these themes. In 1991, Candy sorted out the literature up to that point and developed a helpful framework. The four facets of self-direction he described were learner control (people making decisions about their learning within a formal context), autonomy (a personal characteristic), self-management (planning one's educational experiences), and autodidaxy (engaging in informal, independent learning projects).

Many writers propose that adult learning should be practical or *experiential* in nature, an idea that began with Dewey (1938) and has stayed with us over the decades. It is based on the assumption that adults have immediate problems to solve and that they wish to apply their learning directly to their workplace or to their personal lives. Most surveys of why adults participate in educational programs reveal this as a theme (Livneh & Livneh, 1999), practitioners make every effort to include real-life applications in their programs, and acting on learning (or sometimes "transfer of learning," meaning application in the world outside of the classroom) is often described as the goal of education. Mezirow (2003b) suggests that transformation has not taken place until an individual has acted on the learning. However, as I propose in Chapter Five, people may vary on the extent to which they value practical learning and experiential activities.

Through the influence of humanism, we tend to see adult education as *collaborative* and participatory. Sitting in a circle, working in groups, and interacting with others are hallmarks of adult education practice. Educators describe themselves as facilitators rather than teachers, and they seek to establish a co-learner role with their students. They consider a comfortable and safe atmosphere, both physical and psychological, to be important. Recent explorations of critical theory and postmodernism in adult education have called some of these assumptions into question. Brookfield (2001), for example, uses Foucault's understanding of power to point out how many of our traditional collaborative approaches, such as sitting in a circle, lead people to feel vulnerable and exposed, and other techniques, such as keeping a personal journal, actually allow the educator to engage in surveillance or "get into the head" of the participant.

Knowles (1980), whose work still forms the foundation of much of what we do in adult education today, emphasized the rich *experiences and resources* adults bring to the learning setting. If we disagree with all of the other characteristics that distinguish andragogy (defined by Knowles as the art and science of helping adults learn) from pedagogy, we cannot deny that adults have more experience to bring than do children. From a constructivist point of view, learners share their experiences and resources with each other to create new knowledge. This tenet fits well with the other defining qualities of adult learning—the learning is practical and relevant, people collaborate to construct learning, it is voluntary, and to some extent at least, it must be self-directed. We can question, of course, whether sharing experiences is important to all individuals and whether all types of learning are enhanced by this process.

Self-concept is frequently mentioned in relation to adult learning. A low self-concept is seen as inhibiting learning, and increased self-concept is described as a goal of adult learning. This is certainly also related to the prevailing notion that the climate of adult classes should be comfortable, safe, and relaxing. Along the same lines, there is the worry that going "back to school," especially engaging in formal educational activities, is *anxiety-provoking* for adults. This follows from the assumption that school was a negative, teacher-directed experience for many, and a return to this atmosphere brings back the fears of earlier years. Another line of reasoning here is that many adults have been away from learning experiences for a number of years and have rusty reading, writing, and time management skills, which lead them to feel anxious about their ability to succeed. In the last decade or two, as people make more and more shifts in their careers and retraining and professional development become more common, this characteristic may be less defining of adult learning than it was in previous times.

Discussions of adult learning almost always include mention of *learning styles*. Those who specialize in childhood education also are concerned with learning style, so this characteristic does not necessarily differentiate adult from childhood learning. Cognitive style refers to how people acquire, process, store, and use information, and there are a number of different approaches to defining cognitive style

(Cranton, 2000b). Learning style consists of a preference for a certain condition or way of learning and is generally considered to be value-neutral (MacKeracher, 2004); that is, one style is not better than another. Kolb's (1984) delineation of convergers, assimilators, divergers, and accommodators remains popular today. More recently, we have been influenced by Gardner's (Gardner, Kornhaber, & Wake, 1996) idea of multiple intelligences (musical, bodily-kinesthetic, logical-mathematical, linguistic, spatial, interpersonal, intrapersonal, and natural) and Goleman's (1998) notion of emotional intelligence. The latter has to do with a person's ability to manage emotions, recognize emotions in others, and establish good relationships with others. Some associate learning preferences to gender. For example, MacKeracher (2004), among others, suggests that women prefer relational learning and men autonomous learning. This can also be seen as stereotyping and marginalizing women (English, 2004).

Transformative Learning in Context

If I have succeeded in describing some of the features of adult learning as they have been presented in the literature over the last two or three decades, and I am not sure I have, how does transformative learning fit within this context? I now go back over the characteristics with an eye specifically turned to transformative learning.

There seems to be no doubt that transformative learning is voluntary. People may not always deliberately set out to critically question their beliefs and values; many times transformative learning is prompted by an outside event and that event may be unexpected, hurtful, or devastating. Even so, people have the choice of being critically self-reflective or not. In a classroom or other learning environment where the educator has fostering transformative learning as a goal, participants still voluntarily engage in the process. If someone were to mandate transformation or try to force people into the process, I think we step outside of the definition of transformative learning and into something like brainwashing or indoctrination.

Is transformative learning self-directed? I see the two concepts as interwoven. If we agree that transformative learning is voluntary, as I have just proposed, then a certain amount of self-direction is required for an individual to take the steps of moving into a critical questioning of beliefs, assumptions, and perspectives. People who are completely oppressed may not have the ability to move into this process for all sorts of personal and social reasons. (This is one of the criticisms of Mezirow's work by those who advocate transformative learning as social change.) Mezirow (2000) says that those who are hungry and living in poverty or other extreme social conditions are not likely to participate in transformative learning. Merriam (2004) goes so far as to propose that people need a certain level of cognitive development, and hence a certain level of education. Although these statements are certainly questionable, especially when we are open to processes other than critical self-reflection as central to transformation, it still seems to be the case that transformative learning leads to increased self-direction, so in a way the two go hand in hand. Both are developmental processes.

If being practical or experiential is a defining characteristic of adult learning in terms of adults having immediate problems they wish to solve (and I am not sure this is always the case—people come to learning for a variety of reasons), transformative learning does not necessarily meet this prerequisite. True, it is often provoked by an experience, and Kolb (1984) among others sees reflection on experience as a necessary part of learning, but the process itself may be driven by critical *self*-reflection, exploration, and intuition with no further reference to the world outside of the self. This may be especially true for more introverted people (see Chapter Five) and in those times when transformation involves unconscious images and soul work (Dirkx, 2000). Discourse with others may play a vital role, and at times, transformative learning may look like problem solving, but I do not see it necessarily as being a practical process. If we follow Mezirow's thinking, the outcome should be action, but the learning process need not be experiential.

That adult learning in general is seen as participatory and collaborative applies to some extent to transformative learning, depending on how one views the theory. Belenky and Stanton (2000), for example, emphasize conflicts being resolved through dialogue, conversation, storytelling, and perspective sharing. Mezirow (2000) sees discourse with others as playing an important role in transformative learning. The sharing of experiences and values within a comfortable group atmosphere can obviously act as a stimulant for critical questioning. However, transformation can also occur without collaboration, so I do not think we can describe collaboration as being a defining characteristic of transformative learning.

Transformative learning has to do with making meaning out of experiences and questioning assumptions based on prior experience. Our habitual expectations—what we expect to happen based on what has happened in the past—are the product of experiences, and it is those expectations that are called into question during the transformative learning process. If adult learning is distinguished from childhood learning by the experiences people bring to it, then so can transformative learning be explained as a prerogative of adults. Mezirow (2000) draws on King and Kitchener (1994) and others to argue that it is only in adulthood that people develop the reflective judgment necessary to assess their own reasoning about their habitual expectations.

Self-concept is as relevant to transformative learning as it is to adult learning in general. By definition, transformative learning leads to a changed self-perception. When people revise their habits of mind, they are reinterpreting their sense of self in relation to the world. I think of the college trades instructors with whom I work every summer in the Maritimes of Canada. They have returned to school after years and sometimes decades of experience in their trade, and they are in the process of becoming teachers of their trade. Their self-concept in relation to their ability to succeed in university courses may be shaky, but they have chosen to teach, and this is something they must do. At the same time, they are confident and sure of their skills as electricians, carpenters, and automotive mechanics. How they see themselves and how they come to see themselves over the course of this transition is often transformative. Their self-concept is central to the process they undergo.

Although it is not often mentioned in the transformative learning literature, I see learning style as an important consideration in understanding how people experience transformation. I have long advocated for an expansion of the description of transformative learning that is open to this (Cranton, 1994; 2000a). I explore this more fully in Chapter Five.

Perspectives on Adult Learning

There are many patterns or systems of understanding adult learning. Merriam and Brockett (1997) present a philosophical classification system that includes liberalism, progressivism, behaviorism, humanism, and radicalism. The oldest philosophy in Western society is liberal education where the goal is to produce "intelligent, informed, cultured, and moral citizenry" (p. 33). In the mid-nineteenth century, progressivism emerged in response to industrialization. In this philosophy, more emphasis is placed on knowledge derived from science and rationality, and experience is seen as a source of learning. The behaviorists of the 1950s saw learning as a change in behavior that occurs as people respond to stimuli from the environment and are rewarded or punished. Knowledge is seen to be external to the self. Humanist philosophies came forward in reaction to behaviorism, although the roots of this way of thinking are much older. The humanists of the 1960s viewed learning as personal development through interpersonal relationships which, in turn, contributes to the common good of humanity. The radical or critical philosophical framework of education came to the fore in the late 1960s and early 1970s through the work of Paulo Freire and Ivan Illich. The goal is social change through challenges to the current capitalist and democratic systems. Feminist theory has also contributed to the thinking of radical educators.

It may be helpful to think of there being at least two dimensions underlying the different perspectives on adult learning. One is the individual-to-social continuum. Some theorists and some practitioners prefer to focus on the individual's learning process, while others are more interested in social change and advocating for reform. Humanists tend to be interested in individual development and critical theorists in social reform. Transformative learning can be viewed from either perspective (Brookfield, 2000), and, indeed, this is a debate in the literature. Perhaps it need not be an either-or issue, but simply a preference as to where educators wish to spend their time and energy. Both individual and social perspectives are important, and obviously both exist, one within the other. We become individuals in a society.

The second dimension has to do with kinds of knowledge—the interests that drive the learning process and the type of knowledge that results from the learning. This is not a continuum, but rather a set of interrelated understandings of the world and ourselves within that world (in that sense, the individual-social continuum exists within kinds of knowledge). It is helpful, in locating transformative learning within the larger arena of adult learning theory, to see how it is connected to the different kinds of knowledge with which educators work. Does a trades instructor have the potential to foster transformative learning? A literacy educator? A teacher of nursing? There are many ways of classifying knowledge, as anyone who has ventured into philosophy can attest. Here, I use Habermas's (1971) work, and I choose this foundation as it is one Mezirow (1991) drew upon when he introduced transformative learning theory to the adult education literature.

Technical Knowledge

Technical knowledge is that which allows us to manipulate and control the environment, predict observable physical and social events, and take appropriate actions. Empirical or natural scientific methodologies produce technically useful knowledge, the knowledge necessary for industry and production in modern society. In this paradigm, knowledge is established by reference to external reality, using the senses. There is an objective world made up of observable phenomena. The laws governing physical and social systems can be identified through science, and these systems are seen to operate independently of human perceptions. Habermas criticizes instrumental rationality when it becomes such a pervasive ideology that we either believe all knowledge is instrumental or try to fit all knowledge into that category. In the Age of Enlightenment, the application of reason was seen as the way to solve the world's problems. As a result, empirical scientific methods were viewed as superior to subjective, qualitative, or spiritual ways of knowing. Only recently has modernism (the reign of logic) been criticized in the social sciences and education as not allowing a deeper, more open understanding of human interactions.

Mezirow (1991) refers to the acquisition of technical knowledge as instrumental learning. Much of adult education practice has instrumental learning as a goal. Workplace programs often consist of training and retraining programs that focus on instrumental learning. Trades and technology programs contain both theoretical and practical, hands-on learning in concrete areas such as marine or automobile mechanics, silviculture, dental hygiene, and electronic communications. A good proportion of professional development for health professionals emphasizes new scientific information and techniques. However, problems arise when areas such as interpersonal relations and communications are treated as instrumental learning and forced into the training model.

Practical Knowledge

The second kind of knowledge is based on our need to understand each other through language. Habermas (1971) calls this practical or communicative knowledge. Human beings have always been social creatures, instinctively forming groups, tribes, communities, cultures, and nations in order to satisfy their mutual needs. In order for people to survive together in groups and societies, they must communicate with and understand each other. There are no scientific laws governing these communications—when we communicate with others, we interpret what they say in our own way. This does not mean that communicative knowledge is entirely individual. All societies share and transmit social knowledge, that is, a code of commonly accepted beliefs and behavior. As a society we come to agree on how things should be and are in reference to standards and values, moral and political issues, educational and social systems, and government actions. Communicative knowledge is derived from shared interpretation and consensus and then often becomes reified. Habermas criticizes communicative knowledge as being too dependent on subjective understanding. He argues that people may misinterpret the world around them based on distorted assumptions about themselves or society. We want social knowledge to be objective and concrete and therefore stop questioning the systems around us, unaware of the distortions that may exist in our assumptions.

It is fairly obvious that the acquisition of practical or communicative knowledge comprises a good deal of what people do in adult education. Studies in psychology, sociology, politics, education, language, literature, fine arts, and history focus on communicative learning. Leadership training, interpersonal skills, teamwork, conflict resolution, communication skills, and the new emphasis on emotional intelligence illustrate the importance of communicative learning in workplace settings. Almost wherever you see people working collaboratively in groups to share and interpret their experiences and construct new understandings, you have communicative learning taking place.

Emancipatory Knowledge

The third kind of knowledge, which derives from a questioning of instrumental and communicative knowledge, Habermas calls emancipatory. By nature, people are interested in self-knowledge, growth, development, and freedom. Gaining emancipatory knowledge is dependent on our abilities to be self-determining and self-reflective. Self-determination can be described as the capacity to both be aware and critical of ourselves and of our social and cultural context. Self-reflection involves being aware and critical of our subjective perceptions of knowledge and of the constraints of social knowledge. Emancipatory knowledge is gained through a process of critically questioning ourselves and the social systems within which we live. The philosophical foundation of emancipatory knowledge lies in critical theory. In this paradigm, instrumental and communicative knowledge are not rejected but are seen as limiting. If we do not question current scientific and social theories and accepted truths, we may never realize how we are constrained by their inevitable distortions and errors. Without the possibility of critical questioning of ourselves and our beliefs, such constraining knowledge can be accepted by entire cultures.

Emancipatory learning has been a goal of adult education through time and, to some extent, across cultures. In a history of adult education in Britain, Harrison (1961) states that "it has been in the main regarded as a movement for freedom and liberation, both personal . . . and social" (p. xii). In North America, Lindeman (1926) describes ideal adult education as cooperative, nonauthoritarian, informal, and as a quest for the roots of our preconceptions. Freire (1970) saw his work in literacy education in South America as a "deepening awareness of both the sociocultural reality which shapes [learners'] lives and . . . their capacity to transform that reality through action upon it" (p. 27).

A careful reading of Mezirow's (1991) expression of the goal of adult education as transformative learning reveals how it is drawn from Habermas's idea of emancipatory knowledge and also reflects the thinking of earlier theorists: "The goal of adult education is to help adult learners become more critically reflective, participate more fully and freely in rational discourse and action, and advance developmentally by moving toward meaning perspectives that are more inclusive, discriminating, permeable, and integrative of experience" (pp. 224–225). There have been variations in wording and debates about the role of critical reflection and discourse in the process, but the essence of this statement has remained at the core of transformative learning theory.

Emancipatory learning occurs in informal and formal educational settings, including community development groups, self-help groups, professional development programs, literacy education, union education, and political and environmental movements, to name just a few. Perhaps more important, emancipatory learning can occur in any setting where learning occurs. A person acquiring a technical skill can gain new self-confidence and begin to see his or her place in the world in a new light. When I first learned Blackboard and WebCT (software programs for online teaching), I acquired instrumental knowledge, but I revised my perspective on what good education is as a result. In some of the great social change movements in adult education, such as the Antigonish movement in Canada (for example, see Gillen, 1998), people obtained basic economic, literacy, and social skills, which provided them with the foundation for emancipatory learning.

Perspectives on Adult Learning: Integration

Now that I have taken apart the different kinds of learning in order to see what place transformative learning has, I would like to put them back together again before we proceed to the next chapters. I find it useful to categorize things in order to understand them, but I also find it limiting and fragmenting to leave these things in their categories.

Let us think about Steve's learning. I worked with Steve in a recent summer school program, and although I have changed information that might identify him, the story follows his journey. Steve is a marine mechanic in his late forties. Steve has come to the university to work on a Certificate in Adult Education in hopes of finding a position teaching his trade. Steve's hands bear the marks of his years in his trade—they look swollen and stiff, and the black of engine grease seems worn into his skin. He dresses in jeans and a T-shirt, even though most of the other men in the group wear shorts during the hot summer days (our classroom has no air conditioning). Steve is friendly, he smiles often, and he is quiet in class.

Steve is nervous about a good many things, as can be imagined. For our purposes here, I am going to concentrate on just one of those things—his need to acquire a variety of technical computer skills. Steve had struggled through one online course, impeded by his poor keyboarding and his lack of familiarity with computers, and he had been learning to use e-mail and e-mail attachments. In our course, he decided to participate in a blog (Web-based dialogue) learning activity with a classmate. When a few others in the group offered to teach PowerPoint to those who were interested, Steve was enthusiastic about this opportunity as well. He was not sure as to how these skills would be useful in his future teaching career, but he felt they were things he should know.

Steve's acquisition of the technical skills required to participate in the blog and to create a PowerPoint presentation occurs with a mixture of joy, anxiety, and, I sense, a feeling of being an imposter. What is he doing here? How do all of these things fit together? Should he be in a university course? How can he contribute to others' learning in the way his classmates are contributing to his? It would be impossible, I think, to separate Steve's instrumental learning from his communicative learning. As he participates in the blog activity, the technique skills he learns are simultaneously applied to dialogue with his peer and me. It is not that he learns something and then uses it later in a different way—the two occur together.

To learn PowerPoint, we are all together in a computer lab and three of the course members lead the learning. I am participating as a learner, but I notice how it is going with Steve and other newcomers to this technology. Again, the technical skill is learned and simultaneously used to create something that communicates with others. Steve is excited; he shares his work with those near him, and he looks around, laughing.

I can see the two strands—instrumental and communicative learning—but I cannot see how they could be separated. And what of the emancipatory learning? Steve questioned his assumptions about who he was and what he was capable of doing and revised his self-perception in such a way that it was more open and better justified (I also had the opportunity to read his autobiography and his reflections on the course, which supported my observations of his learning). He became free of some fairly overwhelming constraints stemming from his past habits of mind. Of course, I cannot attribute all of this to his participating in a blog or learning PowerPoint, but neither can I separate it from that learning. In his final reflection and self-evaluation, Steve said that "everything came together," and he saw how he "could be a teacher." Things were no longer "little pieces," "the whole made sense." In this way, meaningful learning integrates instrumental and communicative knowledge, and emancipatory learning occurs when that knowledge changes a person's perspective on himself and the world.

Steve's story is not representative, of course, of all learning experiences, though I see it often enough to be sure that it is not unique either. Still, there are times when people go along acquiring large amounts of instrumental or communicative knowledge before the pieces come together, and there are many occasions when emancipatory learning does not occur. As Mezirow (2000) says, learning can also be the acquisition of new knowledge or elaboration on existing knowledge without calling into question any previously held assumptions or beliefs. However, as educators I think we should always be conscious of the potential of those moments when the acquisition of new knowledge can move into the realm of emancipation. In order to do this, we need to be aware of the wholeness of learning. As useful as it would appear to be on the surface to be able to say "this is going to be transformative learning" and "this cannot be transformative," I think we would do ourselves a disservice to try to define this out of context. We know that transformative learning involves a deep shift in perspective and that it leads to a way of seeing the world that is more open. But we cannot say what kind of a learning experience will promote this shift in perspective in any person or any context.

Summary

In the last ten or fifteen years, transformative learning theory has taken a central place in the adult education literature. There are conferences and a journal dedicated solely to transformative learning. In this chapter, I situate transformative learning within the broader field. I do this in two ways. First, I review some of the key features that are used to characterize adult learning—the voluntary nature of adult learning, adults' preference for self-direction, the importance of adult learning meeting practical needs, its collaborative nature, the role of adults' experiences in their learning, the relevance of self-concept, and the emphasis on learning styles. Although not all of these characteristics are unique to the learning of adults, together they provide an overall description of how we think of adult learning. I explore how each of these qualities is an attribute of transformative learning.

Second, I look at different perspectives on adult learning, starting with a brief overview of philosophies of adult learning. I think there are at least two dimensions underlying the way we see adult learning—the individual-social continuum and the kinds of knowledge we are interested in. I discuss this latter dimension in more depth using Habermas's three types of knowledge (from which Mezirow found a basis for transformative learning theory). *Technical knowledge* is the cause-and-effect, objective, scientific knowledge that allows us to control and manipulate our environment. *Practical* or *communicative knowledge* is the knowledge of ourselves, others, and our social world. *Emancipatory knowledge* is that which frees us from personal and social constraints and leads to awareness and development. It is emancipatory learning, which is based on the critical examination of instrumental and communicative knowledge, that is transformative.

Finally, I argue that any classification system is limiting, and propose that we often cannot separate kinds of learning. I illustrate this with the story of Steve, whose acquisition of instrumental and communicative knowledge occurs simultaneously with his emancipatory learning. Transformative learning is a subset of adult learning—not all adult learning is transformative—but it does not occur separately from other kinds of learning. It is when instrumental and communicative learning leads us to question our previously held views about ourselves and the world around us that the potential for transformative learning exists.

2

Transformative Learning Theory

Throughout their lifetime, people make meaning out of their experiences. They build a way of seeing the world, a way of interpreting what happens to them, and accompanying values, beliefs, and assumptions that determine their behavior. Much of this framework is uncritically absorbed from family, community, and culture. People do not stop to question everything that happens to them or everything they see and hear—they generally believe their friends, accept media interpretations of events, and follow the principles that have guided them so far. People have a set of expectations about the world that are based on formative childhood experiences, and those expectations continue to act as a filter for understanding life.

When something unexpected happens, when a person encounters something that does not fit in with his or her expectations of how things should be, based on past experience, the choices are to reject the unexpected or to question the expectation. When people critically examine their habitual expectations, revise them, and act on the revised point of view, transformative learning occurs. Transformative learning leads to perspectives that are more inclusive, discriminating, and integrative of experience (Mezirow, 2000).

In this chapter, I briefly outline how transformative learning theory developed from 1975 to the present and then turn to a full description of the theory. I use Mezirow's work as the foundation for the description in this chapter, and I explore alternatives in Chapter Three.

Development of Transformative Learning Theory

Based on a study of eighty-three women returning to college in twelve different reentry programs, Mezirow (1975) initially described a process of personal perspective transformation that included ten phases:

- Experiencing a disorienting dilemma

- Undergoing self-examination

- Conducting a critical assessment of internalized assumptions and feeling a sense of alienation from traditional social expectations

- Relating discontent to the similar experiences of others—recognizing that the problem is shared

- Exploring options for new ways of acting

- Building competence and self-confidence in new roles

- Planning a course of action

- Acquiring the knowledge and skills for implementing a new course of action

- Trying out new roles and assessing them

- Reintegrating into society with the new perspective

It is interesting to note that six of the ten phases have to do with preparation for and implementation of new, revised perspectives. In recent years, the emphasis has been much more on encountering the disorienting event and critically questioning or responding to the assumptions and expectations that make it disorienting.

The results of Mezirow's research led him to outline a theory of adult development, which he called perspective transformation—"a structural reorganization in the way that a person looks at himself and his relationships" (Mezirow, 1978, p. 162).

In 1981, Mezirow drew on Habermas's (1971) three kinds of learning (see Chapter One) in order to construct what he called a critical theory of adult learning and education. Mezirow equated emancipatory action with perspective transformation in this writing. At this time, he was interested in "psycho-cultural assumptions" (Mezirow, 1981, p. 6)—the way in which a person's past constrains perceptions of the self and relationships with others.

In 1985, Mezirow elaborated on his concept of perspective transformation and related it to self-directed learning. He saw learning as a process of making assumptions explicit, contextualizing them, validating them, and acting on them. Education was the process of fostering this effort, and self-directedness was the ability to understand our own experiences. He described a self-directed learner as one who participates freely in dialogue in order to test perspectives against those of others and modify them accordingly (Mezirow, 1985b). In other words, a self-directed learner was one who engaged in transformative learning. At this time, too, meaning perspectives were defined as the structure or web of cultural and psychological assumptions, and meaning schemes as the rules and expectations that govern our lives (Mezirow, 1985a, p. 144).

Mezirow's use of Habermas's work was criticized as being inaccurate, and in response, he suggested that emancipatory learning was not a separate domain, but rather, applicable to both instrumental and communicative learning (Mezirow, 1989). In 1990, he edited *Fostering Critical Reflection in Adulthood,* in which he gathered together several authors' diverse perspectives on how critical reflection and hence transformative learning could be fostered. But it was his 1991 book, *Transformative Dimensions of Adult Learning,* which brought the theory to the forefront of the adult education literature. This work was criticized for not including issues to do with social action, power, and cultural context. It was also judged as being too rational, thereby ignoring the role of intuition, symbols, and images in learning. Mezirow invited and encouraged critiques of his work, hoping that within the community of educators interested in transformative learning, the theory would continue to evolve. However, he maintained his stance that the process of transformation was a cognitive rational one: "Transformative learning is understood as a uniquely adult form of metacognitive reasoning. Reasoning is the process of advancing and assessing reasons, especially those that provide arguments supporting beliefs resulting in decisions to act. Beliefs are justified when they are based on good reasons" (Mezirow, 2003a, p. 58).

In 2000, Mezirow edited *Learning as Transformation: Critical Perspectives on a Theory in Progress*, based in part on papers presented at the 1998 International Transformative Learning Conference (Mezirow and Associates, 2000). In his own chapter in this volume, Mezirow acknowledges the importance of the affective, emotional, and social context aspects of transformative learning. He also agrees that there are "asymmetrical power relationships" (p. 28) in the learning process. Other chapters present diverse points of view on transformative learning such as Daloz's (2000) developmental approach and Belenky and Stanton's (2000) concept of connected knowing. I elaborate on the additions to Mezirow's cognitive-rational approach in Chapter Three.

Around this same time, Mezirow (2000) introduced some new terminology—habits of mind and points of view. He described a frame of reference as the web of assumptions and expectations through which we filter the way we see the world. A frame of reference has two dimensions—a habit of mind and the resulting points of view. Habits of mind are the broad predispositions that we use to interpret experience. A habit of mind is expressed as a point of view. A point of view is a cluster of meaning schemes, and meaning schemes are habitual, implicit rules for interpreting experiences.

Overview of Transformative Learning Theory

Transformative learning theory is based on constructivist assumptions. In other words, meaning is seen to exist within ourselves, not in external forms. We develop or construct personal meaning from our experience and validate it through interaction and communication with others. What we make of the world is a result of our perceptions of our experiences. If we were to claim the existence of absolute truths or universal constructs that are independent of our knowledge of them, the goal of learning would be to discover the right answers rather than to reflect on our perspectives of the world. Transformative learning is a process of examining, questioning, validating, and revising our perspectives. In 2003a, Mezirow writes, "Transformative learning is learning that transforms problematic frames of reference—sets of fixed assumptions and expectations (habits of mind, meaning perspectives, mindsets)—to make them more inclusive, discriminating, open, reflective, and emotionally able to change. Such frames of reference are better than others because they are more likely to generate beliefs and opinions that will prove more true or justified to guide action" (pp. 58–59).

Our experiences are filtered through our meaning perspectives or habits of mind, which include uncritically assimilated ways of knowing, believing, and feeling. They include distortions, prejudices, stereotypes, and simply unquestioned or unexamined beliefs. Maintaining a meaning perspective is safe.

Learning occurs when an individual encounters an alternative perspective and prior habits of mind are called into question. Mezirow originally saw this as a single, dramatic event—a disorienting dilemma—but he and others (Mezirow, 2000; E. Taylor, 2000a) have since acknowledged that it could also be a gradual cumulative process. Mezirow (2000) describes transformative learning that is stimulated by a dramatic event as epochal and that which is more gradual as incremental. Dirkx (2000) proposes that transformative learning is more often a process of everyday occurrences than it is a "burning bush" phenomenon.

If a person responds to an alternative habit of mind by reconsidering and revising prior belief systems, the learning becomes transformative. As Mezirow (1991) puts it, "reflective learning becomes transformative whenever assumptions or premises are found to be distorting, inauthentic, or otherwise invalid" (p. 6).

In all of Mezirow's writing, discourse is central to transformative learning. He defines discourse as dialogue involving the assessment of beliefs, feelings, and values (Mezirow, 2003a, p. 59). Under ideal conditions (which cannot be established completely), participants in discourse will

- Have accurate and complete information

- Be free from coercion and distorting self-perception

- Be able to weigh evidence and assess arguments objectively

- Be open to alternative perspectives

- Be able to reflect critically on presuppositions and their consequences

- Have equal opportunity to participate

- Be able to accept an informed, objective consensus as valid (Mezirow, 1991, p. 78)

Types of Habits of Mind

Mezirow (1991) originally distinguished between three kinds of meaning perspectives: epistemic, sociolinguistic, and psychological, but he has since expanded this to include six habits of mind (Mezirow, 2000). He does not see these categories as independent, but rather as overlapping and influencing each other. A habit of mind is a way of seeing the world based on our background, experience, culture, and personality. Since all of our habits of mind are determined by our personal story, it is reasonable to expect that they are interrelated.

Epistemic habits of mind are those related to knowledge and the way we acquire and use knowledge. For more than two decades, I had deeply held convictions about the nature of teaching as involving face-to-face communication. When I reluctantly engaged in online teaching, I was pushed into questioning that perspective, a process that led to a fundamental shift in my knowledge about teaching. When Steve (in Chapter One) learned how to use PowerPoint, it was not only a technical skill that he acquired, but a revision to his epistemic assumptions about teaching—his knowledge about teaching.

Epistemic habits of mind are also about the way we learn—learning styles and preferences. Whether a person thinks globally or in detail, concretely or abstractly, or in an organized or intuitive way forms epistemic perspectives that are influenced by those preferences. We do not easily change the way we learn. These preferences are very much about who we are as human beings; they are long-held and deeply valued ways of seeing ourselves. For me to move away from my analytical approach to understanding theory, for example, seems almost impossible, and I only catch glimpses of how it might be to approach learning in different ways.

Sociolinguistic habits of mind are based on social norms, cultural expectations, and the way we use language. Media images of war and violence form our perceptions of violence. Phrases and slogans such as "weapons of mass destruction" lead our thinking in ways we may not be conscious of. Growing up in a culture in which women's roles are clearly defined as submissive shape our habits of mind about how women should behave. Having limited exposure to cultural differences could lead us to be fearful of or antagonist toward diversity.

In a panel presentation at the American Educational Research Conference, the authors Brookfield, Sheared, Johnson-Bailey, and Colin (2005) probe the dominant, mainstream perspectives on race through a sharing of experiences and stories. The constructs are deep and unconsciously absorbed. White adult educators cannot enter the world of their colleagues of color, and even attempting to do so can paradoxically emphasize their privilege. It is no simple matter to bring our sociolinguistic habits of mind to the forefront of consciousness and consider them in a way that has the potential to lead to transformation.

Psychological habits of mind have to do with how people see themselves—their self-concept, needs, inhibitions, anxieties, and fears. Feeling unloved as a child could lead to feeling unworthy as an adult. Someone whose parents had very high expectations of achievement in school may develop a perspective that includes great motivation to achieve or possibly a sense of guilt about never being able to achieve enough. The sources of psychological habits of mind are often buried in childhood experiences, including trauma, and may not be easily accessible to the conscious self.

Personality traits also comprise a facet of our psychological habits of mind (see Chapter Five). Whether we prefer to make judgments by using thinking or feeling, whether we have an introverted or extraverted attitude toward the world, and whether we perceive the world through our senses or through our intuition act as filters in the way we see the world.

Moral-ethical habits of mind incorporate conscience and morality. How people define good and evil, how they act on their views of goodness, and the extent to which they see themselves as responsible for advocating for justice in the world create a perspective for making meaning out of the world. People donate time and money to charitable organizations, protest against war, boycott products and services, and stop to help a neighbor based on moral-ethical habits of mind.

Brookfield (2005), in his discussion of Habermas's view of social evolution, explains that "the development of morality is indicated by people's ability to detach themselves from everyday thinking and decide (after participating in discussions with others about the ethical justifications of various approaches to situations) how to act in ways that are not ideologically predetermined" (p. 257). Individuals can develop a moral consciousness that is of a higher stage than that which is embodied in the institutions of society.

Philosophical habits of mind can be based on a transcendental worldview, philosophy, or religious doctrine. Most religious systems contain a complex web of values, beliefs, guides to behavior, and rules for living. The acceptance of a particular religious system, whether it is consciously chosen or assimilated from family, creates a powerful meaning perspective. Everything from style of dress through to political views may be dictated. Philosophical habits of mind based on a worldview are similarly complex. A neighbor of mine, for example, subscribes to a "social credit" worldview, which is described as a "whole orientation to civilization," including the social, political, and economic aspects of living; it calls for a redistribution of wealth, radically different views of employment, the end of capitalism, and so forth.

Aesthetic habits of mind include our values, attitudes, tastes, judgments, and standards about beauty. Aesthetic habits of mind are, in large part, sociolinguistic habits of mind; that is, they are determined by the social norms of the community and culture. Of course, it is possible to be a part of a culture and not hold the same standards about beauty, just as it is possible to reject other subsets of cultural expectations and remain within that culture.

Aesthetic habits of mind may have an even broader meaning. Marcuse (1978), who believes we cannot rely only on our reason, describes powerful aesthetic experiences through art, music, and fiction as having the potential to help people detach themselves from their everyday world and see a fundamentally different point of view. As Brookfield (2005) explains, art gives us "new forms of visual and spoken language and opens us to new ways of sensing and feeling . . . and this is, for Marcuse, the inevitable precursor to social action" (p. 201).

Each of these six kinds of habits of mind is interdependent and interrelated. As helpful as it is to think about different kinds of perspectives, it is just as important to see the interconnections. My way of seeing myself (psychological habit of mind) is influenced by my cultural background (sociolinguistic habit of mind). By growing up in an isolated and poor community that did not value education (sociolinguistic), I ended up with great gaps in my knowledge (epistemic habit of mind). Moral-ethical and aesthetic habits of mind are obviously deeply influenced by sociolinguistic, psychological, and epistemic factors. If, for example, I know little about classical music or art (epistemic perspective), my tastes and standards about beauty (aesthetic perspective) will be very different from those of a person well-informed in the arts. Philosophical habits of mind may provide an umbrella for many other of our perspectives.

Unquestioned Habits of Mind

The way we see the world is a product of our knowledge about the world, our cultural background and language, our psychological nature, our moral and ethical views, the religious doctrine or worldview we subscribe to, and the way we see beauty. Each perspective is made up of interwoven beliefs, values, feelings, and assumptions that together create the lens through which we see the world and form the basis for our actions in the world. That I choose to rescue animals while someone else chooses to kill them reflects our different points of view. That someone protests against an American-led war on Iraq while someone else acts as a suicide bomber illustrates opposing worldviews.

Habits of mind are unexamined. They create limitations and form boxes of which we are unconscious and cannot, therefore, get beyond. In his 1991 book, Mezirow referred to these as distorted meaning perspectives, but the term "distorted" raises questions. If we adhere to a realistic view of the world, then distorted assumptions might be helpful in understanding our stance in relation to that world. However, if we hold a constructivist worldview, we are left with several questions. Who, for example, has the privilege of deciding which perspectives are distorted? If a student finds her perspective to be just fine, can a teacher imply that it is distorted? If a whole community or culture accepts a certain point of view (polygamy is evil, war is necessary), does that mean the view is not distorted? Yet we also do not want to fall into the trap of saying that all opinions and beliefs are equally good and acceptable. It seems that one way through this dilemma is to refer to unquestioned or unexamined rather than distorted habits of mind. This also allows the possibility that once examined, habits of mind do not necessarily need to be abandoned.

Adult developmental theorists give us some help in understanding the characteristics of unquestioned habits of mind. The stage theories of development tend to show a progression of development from simplistic black-and-white perceptions of the world to complex relativistic perceptions. This progression is reflected in Perry's (1970) well-known approach to cognitive development, King and Kitchener's (1994) work on reflective judgment, and Belenky, Clinchy, Goldberger, and Tarule's (1986) work on women's ways of knowing. Since transformative learning is a developmental process, as Mezirow (2004) for example more recently acknowledges, this progression makes sense.

King and Kitchener's (1994) model of reflective judgment contains the following seven stages:

- Beliefs need no justification; what is believed is true.

- Knowledge is absolutely certain but may not be immediately available.

- Knowledge is absolutely certain or temporarily uncertain.

- Knowledge is idiosyncratic; some information may be in error or lost, therefore one cannot know with certainty.

- Knowledge is contextual and subjective; it is available through interpretation.

- Knowledge is constructed by each person and is based on the evaluation of evidence and argument.

- Knowledge is the product of rational inquiry, which is fallible.

Individuals at the earlier stages in the development of reflective judgment are more likely to have unquestioned meaning perspectives. Here are some statements which may be indicative of unexamined assumptions:

- I know the correct procedure for implementing a quality control program because I learned it from the manual I received at a workshop last spring.

- Behaviorist psychology has been proven to be wrong.

- Good teachers are those who clearly state what they expect of students and present information in a well-organized manner.

- In order to get a job as a welder, I must perfect each of the skills on this checklist.

- The war is over; the president said so on the news last night.

- If I can't solve the problem, it's only because I didn't listen carefully enough; every problem has a solution.

- My teacher gave me an A on my practicum so I know I can wire a house.

Some sociolinguistic habits of mind are very difficult to articulate and question. We are deeply embedded in our social world and cannot easily stand outside of it to look at its norms and expectations. Habermas (1984) writes of a system world. Systems, such as a monetary system that has evolved from ownership and the exchange of possessions, have been removed from the realm of individual control. They are no longer questioned or seen as questionable. Rarely do people debate the value of having a legal system, or the necessity of using money as a means of exchange of property, or whether or not educational institutions should exist. We tend to be unaware of the social codes in which power and privilege are distributed. When critical theorists encourage us to deconstruct commonly held points of view and when postmodernists "trouble" or "complicate" beliefs, they are trying to prod these deeply embedded habits of mind.

Mezirow (1991) discusses several ways in which habits of mind become seemingly unquestionable.

- Language-based assumptions are especially insidious, as we need to use language itself to question. Through labeling, we attach the characteristics of the label to the person or thing we have labeled, and when that label is uncritically assimilated, it is hard to call it into question.

- We operate with selective perception. We cannot see and hear everything, so we choose to pay attention to some things and ignore others. It is easier to pay attention to that with which we already agree.

- Drawing on Freire's (1970) levels of consciousness, there are times when people are preoccupied with survival needs, internalize the values of their oppressors, or are impressed with populist leaders. Critical examination of habits of mind is unlikely to occur under those conditions.

- People may have constrained visions of humanity.
  They see humanity as flawed; no amount of reason,
  effort, or action will make a difference (students are
  lazy and not motivated, workers do not care about
  their jobs, the public is stupid and naïve).

Our unquestioned psychological beliefs and assumptions may cause us pain because they are inconsistent with how we prefer to see ourselves as adults. They can be defense mechanisms originating in childhood trauma, mechanisms that are dysfunctional in adulthood (Mezirow, 1991). Those theorists who take a depth psychology approach to transformative learning (Dirkx, 2001b; Scott, 1997, for example) emphasize the power of the unconscious in shaping how we see ourselves. Watkins (2000) describes the unconscious as being made up of clusters of psychic energy or different selves that inform the conscious self. By definition, the unconscious is unexamined and unquestioned. Bringing the unconscious into consciousness is part of what Dirkx (2001a) calls soul work.

In today's society, with the media attention given to physical, sexual, and psychological abuse, we are well aware of the powerful and lifelong impact such tragic experiences can have on people's lives. In these cases, Mezirow's (1991) original term, "distorted assumptions," seems reasonable. It is most often the role of counselors and therapists more so than the role of adult educators to help individuals work through these perspectives.

The source of our unexamined psychological habits of mind can also be more prosaic. Simple childhood experiences that would not necessarily be labeled as traumatic can have a profound impact on self-perception. For example, I think of my well-meaning grandmother who told me that my legs were "big" and therefore she would pay me 25 cents not to wear shorts. To this day, I am uncomfortable in shorts or short skirts and rarely wear them. I am well aware of the source of this perception, but I have not examined it well enough to revise it.

And, of course, past educational experiences, such as childhood school failure and criticism by teachers or peers, can contribute to a person's perception of himself or herself as a learner. Individuals who see themselves as incompetent learners, unable to write or study, and incapable of critical thinking, for example, can likely connect their self-concept to earlier learning experiences.

Types of Reflection

Reflection is a key concept in transformative learning theory. In adult education generally, reflective thinking is a goal of learning. This notion can be traced to Dewey (1933), who defined reflection as "active, persistent and careful consideration of any belief or supposed form of knowledge in the light of the grounds that support it and the further conclusion to which it tends" (p. 9). Current definitions of reflection do not differ substantially from Dewey's understanding. Reflection is still seen as a process of reconsidering experience through reason, and reinterpreting and generalizing the experience to form mental structures (Fenwick, 2000; Mezirow, 2003a).

Mezirow has always maintained that critical reflection is central to transformative learning. In 2003a, he suggests that two distinctively adult learning capabilities are required: the development of a capacity to be critically self-reflective (Kegan, 2000) and to exercise reflective judgment (King and Kitchener, 1994). Mezirow (2003a) writes, "These adult capabilities are indispensable for fully understanding the meaning of our experience and effective rational adult reasoning in critical discourse and communicative learning" (p. 60). Transformative learning requires critical reflection from this perspective.

Although Mezirow no longer emphasizes the distinction among content, process, and premise reflection (Mezirow, 1991), I continue to find this distinction very useful in my practice and thinking about critical reflection, so I include it here.

Content reflection is an examination of the content or description of a problem. It is the equivalent of asking, *What is happening here? What is the problem?* If a learner of automobile mechanics encounters a new piece of equipment for diagnosing fuel injection problems, he or she might ask, "What is this? What does it do? What use might I make of it?" The student could try to determine the characteristics of the equipment, observe someone else using it, or read the manual that came with it. This would form content reflection on a problem related to instrumental knowledge.

In another domain of knowledge, a student returning to an adult education center to obtain her high school equivalency might feel uncomfortable and out of place. She might ask, "What is happening here? What am I feeling?" She could reflect on her reactions to the situation to try to determine whether she is worried about her study skills, feels socially out of place, or is fearful of not being able to succeed. This could be the beginning of a reflective process that would lead to emancipatory learning.

Process reflection involves checking on the problem-solving strategies that are being used. It is asking questions of the form, *How did this come to be?* Let us say that the student of mechanics was unable to immediately identify and use the new piece of equipment. He or she might stop and review the process used so far and ask, "Did I miss something? Do I not understand the manual? Did I misinterpret what my teachers said?" The learner is reflecting on the process of understanding the problem. Similarly, the individual who returns to school and questions her self-perception might ask, "How have I ended up feeling this way? Do I understand myself? Am I overlooking something? How is it that I am unable to adapt?"

Premise reflection takes place when the problem itself is questioned. Reflection takes the form of, *Why is this important to me? Why do I care about this in the first place? What difference does this make? Why is this a problem anyway?* It is an examination of the premise or basis of the problem. The student of mechanics could ask, "Why do I need to operate this equipment? Am I just doing this because someone told me to, or is it really important? Is this just a promotion by the manufacturer? Do I need this?" The learner returning to complete her high school equivalency could ask, "Why am I making this into a problem? Isn't it natural to feel anxious?"

It is premise reflection that has the potential to lead people to the transformation of a habit of mind. Mezirow (1991, 2000) distinguishes between transformative learning that involves the revision of a specific assumption or belief and transformative learning that incorporates the revision of a more complex, wider perspective. Content and process reflection may lead to the transformation of a specific belief, but it is premise reflection that engages learners in seeing themselves and the world in a different way. With premise reflection the student of mechanics could come to see fundamental aspects of the trade differently—how new equipment is introduced and by whom and for what reasons. And with premise reflection, the high school returnee could revise her entire way of reacting to new situations.

In my practice, I find asking reflective questions of these types very useful, as do my students, who are also adult educators. I include more about critical questioning in Chapter Eight and also in other of my writings (for example, see Cranton, 2003). For our purposes here, I include several different forms that content, process, and premise reflection questions might take, depending on the nature of the habit of mind and the kind of knowledge. Exhibit 2.1 includes questions for each of the types of habits of mind, and Exhibit 2.2 contains question formats for Habermas's knowledge domains.

Summary

In the thirty years since Mezirow studied the experiences of women returning to college, transformative learning theory has developed from a ten-step transition model to a complex and comprehensive theory of adult learning. Although Mezirow has remained constant

Exhibit 2.1. Reflective Questions for Habits of Mind.

Reflection	Habit of Mind		
	Psychological	Sociolinguistic	Epistemic
Content	What do I believe about myself?	What are the social norms?	What knowledge do I have?
Process	How have I come to have this perception of myself?	How have these social norms been influential?	How did I obtain this knowledge?
Premise	Why should I question this perception?	Why are these norms important?	Why do I need or not need this knowledge?
	Moral-ethical	Philosophical	Aesthetic
Content	What are my values?	What is my worldview?	What do I find beautiful?
Process	How have my values formed?	How have I come to hold this worldview?	How have my views of beauty been shaped?
Premise	Why are my values important?	Why do I stay with this worldview?	Why do I care about beauty?

in his view that transformation occurs through rational critical self-reflection and discourse, others in the field have elaborated on the ways in which it may occur.

Transformative learning is defined as the process by which people examine problematic frames of reference to make them more inclusive, discriminating, open, reflective, and emotionally able to change. It can be provoked by a single event—a disorienting dilemma—or it can take place gradually and cumulatively over time. Discourse is central to the process. We need to engage in conversation with others in order to better consider alternative perspectives and determine their validity.

Exhibit 2.2. Reflective Questions for Kinds of Knowledge.

Reflection	Knowledge		
	Instrumental	Communicative	Emancipatory
Content	What are the facts?	What do others say about this issue?	What are my assumptions?
Process	How do I know this is true?	How did I integrate others' points of view?	How do I know my assumptions are valid?
Premise	Why is this knowledge important to me?	Why should I believe in this conclusion?	Why should I revise or not my perspective?

Frames of reference are made up of habits of mind (the broad predispositions that we use to interpret experience) and points of view (clusters of meaning schemes, or habitual, implicit rules we use to interpret experience). A habit of mind is expressed as a point of view. If, for example, a person has a habit of mind that predisposes her to admire a strong work ethic, this may be expressed as a point of view in which she is critical of individuals who fraudulently collect unemployment allowances from the government.

Habits of mind may be of different types. Mezirow names at least six overlapping and interrelated habits of mind: epistemic, to do with knowledge and the way we acquire knowledge; sociolinguistic, based on social norms and the way language is used; psychological, to do with how people see themselves; moral-ethical, related to conscience and morality; philosophical, based on worldview or religious doctrine; and aesthetic, including our standards about beauty.

Habits of mind are uncritically absorbed from our family, community, and culture. They tend to remain unquestioned unless we encounter an alternative perspective that we cannot ignore.

Unquestioned habits of mind may be a product of cognitive development, strong societal values, and personal experiences or traumas in childhood.

In Mezirow's view, critical reflection and critical self-reflection are central to transformative learning. In his 1991 book, he delineates three kinds of reflection: content, process, and premise. Content and process reflection (asking "What is the problem?" and "How did this come to be a problem?") may lead to transformation of specific assumptions and beliefs. Premise reflection—challenging the very basis of the problem or issue—has the potential to promote transformation of habits of mind, the web of assumptions and beliefs that acts as a lens through which we see ourselves and the world around us.

3

A Theory in Progress

As is indicated in the subtitle of the book Mezirow edited in 2000, transformative learning theory is a theory in progress. Nowhere is this more evident than in the proceedings of the International Transformative Learning Conferences (for example, see Wiessner, Meyer, Pfhal, and Neuman, 2003). First initiated in 1998 by Victoria Marsick and Jack Mezirow, the purpose of the conference was and continues to be one of expanding and elaborating on transformative learning theory. The book based on the first conference (Mezirow and Associates, 2000) made several of these perspectives accessible to scholars and practitioners in the field.

The earliest critics of transformative learning theory focused on Mezirow's failure to address social change and his selective interpretation of Habermas's work (Collard and Law, 1989), his neglect of power issues (Hart, 1990), his disregard for the cultural context of learning (Clark and Wilson, 1991), and his overemphasis on rational thought (Dirkx, 1997). These issues remain at the center of debates today.

Baumgartner (2001) uses Dirkx's (1998) four-lens approach to understanding the directions in which transformative learning theory has moved. One lens has Freire's (1970) perspective as its foundation; that is, transformative learning can be seen as having liberation from oppression as its goal and social justice as its orientation. The second lens is Mezirow's (2000) concentration on rational thought and reflection as central to a process of responding to a disorienting dilemma, questioning and revising assumptions, engaging in discourse, and acting on a new perspective (see Chapter Two). The third lens is a developmental approach to transformative learning (Daloz, 1999). Here the process is intuitive, holistic, and contextually based; it is a transitional journey that takes place within a social environment. And finally, the fourth lens through which transformative learning can be viewed is one in which learning is linked to spirituality (Dirkx, 2001a, 2001b; Tisdell and Tolliver, 2001). Dirkx describes transformative learning as soul work; other writers link it to specific practices such as Buddhist meditation (Robinson, 2004) and yoga (Cohen, 2003). The popularity of a half-day postconference workshop on spirituality and transformative learning led by Wiessner, Dirkx, and Tisdell at the 2003 International Transformative Learning Conference speaks to the power of this perspective.

In this chapter, I group the directions in which transformative learning theory has developed in a slightly different way, though I do find Dirkx's four lenses very helpful. I first describe the introduction of connected and relational learning into the theory, and I provide some thoughts on transformative learning in relation to social change. These perspectives stretch the basic rationalistic views of Mezirow's theory and open the door for alternative ways of understanding transformative learning, yet they rely primarily on reflection to mediate the learning processes and, in this sense, are an extension of the emphasis on critical reflection described in Chapter Two. I then discuss the application of transformative learning theory to groups and organizations and review how transformative learning can be seen as an approach to worldviews on globalization and environmentalism. I describe the extrarational approach, which represents a fundamental challenge to critical reflection as a way of knowing by suggesting that transformative learning is mediated by unconscious processes beyond the level of rational and conscious awareness. Finally, I summarize some of the research on transformative learning by drawing on E. Taylor's (2000a, 2000b) important reviews and the offerings from both the International Transformative Learning Conferences and the *Journal of Transformative Education*.

Connected Knowing

It is not just in regard to transformative learning theory that there has been considerable debate about whether learning is connected and relational or independent and autonomous (see MacKeracher, 2004, for example). Traditional learning theory focuses on how an individual person learns, and although the context of the learning may be considered, it is generally about that person, not that person learning in and from relationships with others. This sounds odd, given the emphasis on groups and interactive methods in adult education, but learning has long been seen as an individual process even though discussion and group work may be used to get there. Perhaps the roots of this lie in behaviorism, with its emphasis on the individual organism, or perhaps they lie in the models of assessment that drive educational systems. Intelligence and aptitude are always measured individually, and scoring systems are based on comparison and competition among individuals. Evaluation of learning is an individual thing in education from the first grade through to doctoral studies. I have listened to many college instructors agonize over how to grade students when they are engaged in group projects.

Western society values individualism. Every aspect of our life is influenced by this value, including how we think about learning (see for example, Brookfield, 2005). It should not be too big a surprise that we respect autonomous, independent learning. Since Gardner (Gardner, Kornhaber, and Wake, 1996) introduced multiple intelligences, one of which is interpersonal intelligence, and Goleman (1998) brought the concept of emotional intelligence to our attention, there has been some change in our collective perspective. In training programs and workplace education, more emphasis is placed on how people learn to work together. But still, this is primarily about how an individual person learns to work with others, not learn in relation to others.

Feminist writers (Tisdell, 2000a, 2000b) and theorists interested in gender differences in learning (Hayes and Flannery, 2000) emphasize relational or connected learning. Women tend to learn differently, they propose; women learn through relationships with others, through nurturing and caring, and by connecting with each other (Belenky and Stanton, 2000). Belenky and Stanton critique traditional transformative learning theory on this and related bases. They suggest that although Mezirow presumes relations of equality among participants in discourse, most human relationships are asymmetrical. This has serious consequences, especially for women. Dualistic thinking (male-female, thinking-feeling, public-private) serves to create hierarchies in which one pole of the dichotomy is prized and the other devalued. We must, the authors argue, replace dualistic categories with integrative thinking.

Drawing on Belenky's well-known earlier research with her colleagues (Belenky, Clinchy, Goldberger, and Tarule, 1986), Belenky and Stanton (2000) describe six developmental stages of knowing for women: silenced, received knowers, subjective knowers, separate knowers, connected knowers, and constructivist knowers. It is the distinction between separate knowing and connected knowing that is of greatest interest to the authors in examining implications for transformative learning theory. The traditional theory, they suggest, places separate knowing in a central role. Unlike separate knowers, who follow lines of reasoning and look for flaws in logic to create more defensible knowledge, connected knowers suspend judgment and struggle to understand others' points of view from their perspective. They look for strengths not weaknesses in another person's point of view. Belenky and Stanton write, "The more Connected Knowers disagree with another person the harder they will try to understand how that person could imagine such a thing, using empathy, imagination and storytelling as tools for entering into another's frame of mind" (p. 87). They see this as a radically different stance in which the goal is to see holistically, not analytically.

Some recent research validates this understanding of transformative learning. For example, Carter (2000) found that transformation occurred primarily through developmental relationships among the upper-level management women she studied. In describing several types of relationships reported on by her participants, Carter labels one of these as a love relationship—a deep, intimate sharing of experiences and feelings over a sustained period of time. Others of Carter's participants maintained relationships in their memory with loved ones who had died. Gilly (2004) reports on an experience of transformative education among members of a doctoral peer group in which she finds collaboration and relationship to be the central aspects of transformation. In a careful, detailed self-study, J. Clark (2005) dedicates one chapter to the important role of friendship in transformative learning. Clark goes so far as to say that transformative learning could not take place without friendship.

I see some danger in proposing that women engage in transformative learning in one way. To suggest that women learn one way and men another way could be seen as stereotyping, and, given that the way women's learning is depicted is a way that is less valued in our society, this could also serve to further marginalize women. English (2004) speaks well to this issue in reporting on her study of women's learning in volunteer organizations. J. Cohen (2004) describes the stories of transformation in an adult education program that is explicitly designed to incorporate autonomy and connection.

It seems quite reasonable to suggest that different people engage in transformative learning in different ways (see Chapter Five) and that some are more likely to learn through relationships, but I grow cautious when this is drawn along gender lines.

Social Change

Transformative learning theory has long been criticized for not paying enough attention to social change. Although Mezirow (1991, 2000) draws on the works of Freire and Habermas, both of whom have social change as a central goal, Mezirow clearly believes that individual transformation precedes social transformation. Collard and Law (1989), Cunningham (1992), and Hart (1990) were among those who objected to this view early on in the development of the theory.

Social reform has long been a goal of adult education. Two examples come immediately to mind. In Canada, the Antigonish movement was founded by Father Jimmy Tompkins and Father Moses Coady in the late 1920s as a way of helping ordinary people foster economic development through cooperatives and credit unions. Using mass meetings, study groups, kitchen meetings, and community courses, the leaders of the movement sought to "help the people build greater and better democratic institutions" (Coady, 1939, p. 3). The six principles of the Antigonish movement were: (1) individual needs are primary and need to be developed in social contexts, (2) the root of social reform lies in education, (3) individuals are most concerned with economic needs and education must start there, (4) group settings are most suitable to education, (5) social reform both causes and is dependent on change in social and economic institutions, and (6) a full, self-actualized life for everyone in the community is the aim of the movement.

The second example, of course, is the Highland Folk School (now called the Highlander Research and Education Center) founded in the United States by Myles Horton and his colleagues in 1932. As was the case in the Antigonish movement, the goal was to provide education for ordinary people as a way of effecting social change. The development of literacy skills was seen to be one way of fostering both social and personal transformation. Horton's goal was to bring people together to challenge oppressive organizations and governments. Based on interviews with eight current educators from the Highlander Research and Education Center, Ebert, Burford, and Brian (2003) describe nine facets of practice relevant to transformative education: (1) providing a safe place to encourage discourse and reflection, (2) assuming participants bring a wealth of knowledge and experience, (3) helping people discover they are not alone, (4) facilitating critical thinking, (5) helping people develop voice and the confidence to act, (6) solving problems through synergy, (7) encouraging lifelong and diverse learning for change, (8) promoting the idea that everyone is an important member of a community, and (9) implementing continuous improvement.

Writers and theorists who emphasize social action see critical reflection without social action as "a self-indulgent form of speculation that makes no real difference to anything" (Brookfield, 2000, p. 143). Mezirow (2000) distinguishes between educational tasks—helping people become aware of oppressive structures and learn how to change them—and political tasks, which force economic change. This distinction is helpful. It is not the case that Mezirow is saying that social action is not the responsibility of adult educators or the product of transformative learning. He is saying that educators go about making a difference in the world by helping learners learn how to make a difference in the world. Still, this does not fully address the link between transformative learning and social action.

In a review of the work of bell hooks and Angela Davis, Brookfield (2003) concludes that both women see transformative learning as ideology critique. The purpose of transformative education is to "help people uncover and challenge dominant ideology and then learn how to organize social relations according to noncapitalist logic" (p. 224). In social action, disequilibrium is present in all relationships. Transformation includes not only structural change in the individual's way of seeing himself or herself and the world, but also structural change in the social world that provides the context for the individual's life. Newman (1994) places the emphasis solidly on the social structures when he proposes that we should study not the oppressed, but oppression. In his writing on critical theory, Brookfield (2005) takes a similar stance. Ideology critique describes the ways in which people come to recognize uncritically assimilated assumptions and beliefs. The role of adult educators is to help people see how these ideologies (assumptions and beliefs) have been imposed on them without their knowledge and how they justify and maintain economic and political inequity (p. 13).

Merriam and Caffarella (1999) credit both Mezirow and Freire as being the leading theorists in transformative learning, with Freire focusing more on social change than Mezirow. Torres (2003) follows Freire's (1970) view of transformative learning as an instrument for social justice. He raises an interesting paradox. Democracy implies participation based on the assumption of equality among people. Yet people need to be educated in democratic participation. Knowing how to engage in discourse, collaborate with others, and exercise democratic rights and obligations is both a precondition of and a product of democratic participation. Torres argues that "transformative social justice should be based on unveiling the conditions of alienation and exploitation in society, thereby creating the basis for the understanding and comprehension of the roots of social behaviour" (2003, p. 429). He does not, however, deny the importance of what he calls self-transformation, a process by which we rethink our past and gain an understanding of the formation of our self. Understanding our present condition allows us to see the limitations and possibilities of being a "self-in-the-world" (p. 429).

Groups and Organizations

Group and organizational transformation has been a recent line of inquiry. Yorks and Marsick (2000) have focused their research on action learning and collaborative inquiry, two group learning strategies employing reflection and action aimed at producing transformational organizational learning. Similarly, Kasl and Elias (2000) report on transformative learning within the context of group learning and organizational change. It is sometimes difficult to distinguish between transformative learning with social change as a goal and group learning. Scott (2003) helps clarify this when she says that "transformation includes structural changes in the psyches of persons and in the structures of society" (p. 281). Following Kegan's

(2000) constructivist-developmental approach, Scott sees a collective movement occurring toward higher mental functions.

Although learning in groups has a long history in adult education, the idea that a group as an entity can learn is relatively new. Kasl, Marsick, and Dechant (1997) claim that a group, as a system, can create knowledge for itself. The popular work on learning organizations follows this model. The idea began with the work of Argyris and Schön (1974) and was popularized by Senge (1990), among others. But it was the work of Watkins and Marsick (1993) that connected the learning organization to transformative learning. Yorks and Marsick's (2000) work on organizational transformation is based on action learning and collaborative inquiry. Action learning involves learning in small groups or teams by working on a real project or problem in the organization. Collaborative inquiry sounds similar—it is defined as a "process consisting of repeated episodes of reflection and action through which a group of peers strives to answer a question of importance to them" (p. 266). There is an emphasis on co-inquiry, democratic process, and holistic understanding of the experience. According to Yorks and Marsick, organizations transform along several dimensions: the nature of the environment, the vision or mission of the organization, their products or services, the organizational structure, management of the organization, and how members of the organization see their roles.

Fenwick (1998) is quite critical of this perspective. She suggests that those who write about learning organizations are likely to be closely aligned with the organization's goals, but visions and goals of the ordinary person working within the organization may be very different. She also argues that it is not reasonable to describe an organization as a unitary, intelligent entity. It is not unitary, nor is it bounded and stable—it contains multiple subgroups, different cultures, and a continually changing workforce.

Can groups learn and transform? Kasl and Elias's (2000) writing is based on the premise that they can. They use two concepts to support this assumption: that individuals, groups, and organizations all share common characteristics, and the idea of a group mind. Kasl and Elias include both critical reflection and discernment as central processes in their conceptualization of transformative learning. Discernment begins with receptivity and appreciation and moves to seeing patterns of relational wholeness. "Frames of reference are transcended rather than analyzed" (p. 231). Transformative learning becomes an expansion of consciousness that is collective as well as individual. Using a case study, Kasl and Elias illustrate that processes usually ascribed to individuals can provide a model for understanding and interpreting group learning.

Ecological View

O'Sullivan and his colleagues from the Transformative Learning Centre at the Ontario Institute for Studies in Education provide an unusual and intriguing approach to transformative learning. Their broad vision spans the individual, relational, group, institutional, societal, and global perspectives: "Transformative learning involves experiencing a deep, structural shift in basic premises of thought, feelings, and actions. It is a shift of consciousness that dramatically and permanently alters our way of being in the world. Such a shift involves our understanding of ourselves and our self-locations; our relationships with other humans and with the natural world; our understanding of relations of power in interlocking structures of class, race and gender; our body awareness; our visions of alternative approaches to living; and our sense of possibilities for social justice and peace and personal joy" (Transformative Learning Centre, 2004).

O'Sullivan (2003) is careful to say that he does not see transformative learning as an individual process, but rather a personal process that is carried out in "integrally webbed totalities" (p. 337). Central to his understanding is that we are part of the whole. What we should strive for is a planetary community that holds together without collapsing and obliterating human diversity.

In Sweden, the Holma College of Integral Studies takes a similar approach to understanding transformative learning (Gunnlaugson, 2003). The college provides a one-year intensive adult education program in personal and global well-being studies, drawing participants who are looking for personal and collective transformation. An emphasis on "learning to love life in all forms first, then extending this love out from the personal to more universal horizons" (p. 326) allows students to develop what is described as an "integrally informed" education. Gunnlaugson follows O'Sullivan's (2003) thinking in proposing that there is a pressing need to contemplate "our collective evolutional destiny from the vantage point of the history of planet Earth" (p. 324).

Extrarational Approach

It is perhaps the extrarational approach to transformative learning that holds the most promise for expanding the theory, given how different it is from Mezirow's original work. Even though they may not label it as extrarational, many of the new writers in the field are drawn to something beyond the cognitive way of processing (Herman, 2003; Lennard, Thompson, and Booth, 2003). If we can integrate this way of understanding transformation with Mezirow's work rather than treating it as an opposing position, I think we will have made good steps in the direction of developing a unifying, holistic theory (Cranton and Roy, 2003).

Boyd and Myers (1988; Boyd, 1985; Boyd, 1989) were early proponents of using Jungian psychology to explain transformative learning. They describe a process of discernment in which symbols, images, and archetypes play a role in personal illumination. Boyd (1989) reports on a method of working in small groups in which individuals struggle to deal with unconscious content. The group itself affects the way individual members create images, identify personal dilemmas, and relate developmental phases to personal stages. Boyd defines personal transformation as "a fundamental change in one's personality involving conjointly the resolution of a personal dilemma and the expansion of consciousness resulting in greater personality integration" (p. 459). In 1991, Boyd suggests that transformation is an inner journey of individuation, the process of learning through reflection on the psychic structures that make up one's uniqueness. That Boyd's early writing is frequently cited twenty years later shows how it resonates with many people's experience of transformation.

More recently, Dirkx (2001a, 2001b) has taken up the torch of extending transformative learning theory beyond the ego-based, rational, and objective traditional approach. Dirkx (1997) provides the compelling view that transformative learning involves very personal and imaginative ways of knowing—the way of mythos rather than logos. Dirkx draws on Hillman's (2000) and T. Moore's (1996) writings on soul and Jung's ([1921] 1971) concept of individuation.

Transformative learning involves imaginative and emotional ways of knowing, says Dirkx (1997). Mythos reflects a facet of knowing that we can see in symbols, images, stories, and myths. Framing learning as a problem of critical self-reflection leads us to neglect the emotional, spiritual, and imaginative aspects of transformation, and yields a limited, fragmented perspective rather than a holistic, whole-person understanding. Boyd (1991) talks of "transformative education" in order to maintain holism, and similarly, the founders of the *Journal of Transformative Education* chose that title deliberately so as to be inclusive, integrative, and holistic (Markos and McWhinney, 2004).

It is one thing to say this and another to understand what it means in relation to both theory and practice. Dirkx (1997) describes soul through examples of experiences rather than through a definition—being awestruck by a sunset, or gripped by pain and helplessness in the face of another's suffering. We experience soul through art, music, and film. It is that magic moment, defining moment, that transcends rationality and gives depth, power, mystery, and deep meaning to the connection between the self and the world. In nurturing soul, we attend to not only the intellectual aspects of the learning environment, but to the emotional, spiritual, social, and physical aspects as well. We pay attention to the small, everyday occurrences (Dirkx, 2000), listen to individual and collective psyches, understand and appreciate images, and honor the multifaceted dimensions of learning.

Jung ([1921] 1971, p. 448) defines individuation as the process by which individuals differentiate themselves from the general, collective society. It involves becoming aware of and considering the psychic structures of anima, animus, ego, shadow, and the collective unconscious. People come to see how they are both the same as and different from others. Transformation through individuation occurs whether we are conscious of it or not. However, when we participate in it consciously and imaginatively, we develop a deepened sense of self and an expansion of consciousness. Transformation is the emergence of the Self.

The process of individuation, becoming conscious of what is unique about oneself, involves differentiating ourselves from people we have admired and modeled ourselves on—parents, teachers, and mentors (Sharp, 2001). Individuality and group identity are incompatible. According to transformative learning theory, individuals come to question assumptions and perspectives that were uncritically absorbed from family, community, and culture. This sounds very much like differentiating ourselves from others upon whom we have modeled ourselves, except that according to Mezirow, it is a conscious, cognitive, rational, problem-solving process, and according to the Jungian perspective, it is an intuitive, emotional, and often not even a voluntary journey. Jung writes, "The developing personality obeys no caprice, no command, no insight, only brute necessity: it needs the motivating force of inner or outer faculties" (cited in Sharp, 2001, p. 66).

As different as the paths are, it seems they are going to the same place. If we want, as we say we do, a holistic theory of transformative learning, then both paths can be valid. Those among us who strive to develop theories to explain others' learning are also human beings looking at ourselves and the world through the lens of our meaning perspectives. It should not be too surprising that this results in different ways of seeing the journey. Jung ([1921] 1971), in his work on psychological type preferences (see Chapter Five) tells the story of different people taking the same trip. One person may wax eloquently about the beauty of the landscape; another may focus on the restaurants in the area and describe the many good meals he had; someone else may have noticed neither the landscape nor the restaurants, but have spent time getting to know the people and understanding their culture. So it is, I think, with the development of transformative learning theory.

Research on Transformative Learning

With the International Conference on Transformative Learning in its sixth year and the *Journal of Transformative Education* in its third volume, the amount of accessible research on transformative learning has begun to grow exponentially. Prior to the existence of these vehicles for dissemination, much of the research in the area would have been not easily available but for the efforts of E. Taylor (2000a, 2000b), who conscientiously read, summarized, critiqued, and integrated the many graduate theses in the field. In this brief overview of the research, I draw heavily, and with gratitude, on Taylor's work.

Taylor outlines eight themes from the research published up until 2000: (1) transformative learning is uniquely adult; (2) transformative learning appears to be a linear, but not necessarily step-wise process; (3) the nature of a frame of reference and how it transforms is unclear; (4) a disorienting dilemma usually initiates transformative learning; (5) critical reflection is significant to transformative learning; (6) discourse is equally dependent on relational ways of knowing; (7) context plays an important role in shaping transformative learning, but the influence of culture has not been well investigated; and (8) some characteristics of a learning environment that fosters transformative learning have been identified, but more work needs to be done in this area. Essentially, the research supports Mezirow's (2000) theoretical description, with the possible exception of the importance of relational ways of knowing. However, even here, Mezirow (2003a) has now elaborated on the conditions of discourse to include interpersonal skills, social relationships, and emotional intelligence. We must keep in mind that Taylor chose to review only those studies that referred directly to Mezirow's conceptualization of transformative learning, though some studies also included other theoretical models as well.

Based on his review, Taylor suggests future directions for research: (1) in-depth analyses of specific components of transformative learning that tend to be overlooked in the broader studies—for example, feelings such as anger, happiness, and shame, the management of emotions, and changes in behavior following transformation; (2) studies of how transformative learning is fostered in classrooms; and (3) new and varied research designs and data collection techniques, including longitudinal research, observer participation, collaborative inquiry, action research, and quantitative studies.

It is difficult to find research reports that do not, at least in part, have Mezirow's work as a foundation. I include a few examples here, with no intention of providing a comprehensive review. Some of the research on spirituality and transformative learning refers to the work of Dirkx (1997), English and Gillen (2000), and Palmer (1998), for example, rather than to the more cognitive, rational, traditional transformative learning theory. Tisdell (2000b) studied a multicultural group of women adult educators and reports on five themes in their experience: (1) a spiral process of moving beyond the spiritual values of their culture of origin; (2) spirituality as a life force providing interconnectedness and wholeness; (3) the presence of a higher power that facilitates healing and gives courage to take new action; (4) the importance of an integrated and balanced approach to living and a commitment to action for social change; and (5) the development of authentic identity.

I found the latter theme related to authenticity and the integration of personal identity and spirituality to be of special interest in light of my own research. In a study of twenty-two educators over a three-year period, a colleague and I found evidence that the development of an authentic identity as a teacher can be a transformative process (Cranton and Carusetta, 2004b).

Tisdell and Tolliver (2001) later take the results of Tisdell's (2000b) study and explore the implications for transformative learning in adult higher education. They suggest that there has been little discussion of the role of spirituality in teaching for social transformation and propose the importance of (1) the authenticity of teachers and students, (2) an environment that allows for the exploration of the cognitive, the affective or relational, and the symbolic or spiritual dimensions, and (3) the limitations of the adult learning environment and that transformation is an ongoing process that takes time (p. 368).

As I mention earlier in this chapter, Gilly's (2004) research on the nature of a "living learning group" (p. 236) shows the importance of relational, collaborative, and egalitarian group work in transformative learning. The group moved from being a collection of individuals to being a community of practice where the "processes of transforming experience into knowledge were habituated" (p. 236). In relating her study to the literature, Gilly found that the more cognitive rational approach (Cranton, 1994; Mezirow, 2000) did not address important aspects of her experience.

Summary

Transformative learning theory has benefited greatly over the years from the contributions of scholars from a variety of perspectives. Many researchers and writers emphasize relational, connected knowing over individual, autonomous learning. From this perspective, transformative learning has a different emphasis and perhaps a different outcome. Subjective discussion (rather than rational discourse) encourages participants to share their experiences in a non-judgmental way, and connected knowing involves working hard to understand others rather than looking for flaws in others' reasoning.

Social change lies at the heart of the history of adult education. In the 1920s and 1930s, adult education practice and theory was about helping people challenge oppressive organizations and governments. Those who criticize Mezirow's work on the basis of his ignoring social action as a goal of transformative learning may be overlooking his desire to help people learn how to change oppressive structures rather than to change them himself—his distinction between educational and political tasks—as well as overlooking his own commitment to that work. Nevertheless, it is the case that adult education theory in general and transformative learning theory in particular has moved away from social issues and toward an emphasis on individual learning in recent decades. Brookfield's (2005) four traditions of criticality are helpful in understanding how both personal and social transformation are a part of what we do in adult education.

The idea that groups and organizations as entities can learn and transform provides yet another perspective on the theory (Kasl and Elias, 2000). I accept that groups and organizations change and develop, but I question the concept of a "group mind," and therefore I question the idea that groups transform in the way individuals transform. Group transformation is an intriguing idea, but I think it needs to be better situated in transformative learning theory or perhaps named differently.

O'Sullivan's broad vision of transformative learning theory, with its goal of striving for a planetary community, may have the potential of opening up our understanding of transformation so as to integrate all perspectives. I suggest that we need to explore how this vision is related to the existing alternative ways of describing transformation.

The extrarational approach put forth by Dirkx and others provides us with an intriguing and complementary way of understanding the central process of transformation. It brings in imagination, intuition, soul work, and emotion as ways in which people come to see themselves and their world in a new light. As different as the extra-rational approach is from Mezirow's cognitive rational description of transformative learning, the two need not be viewed as contradictory. I do not intend to gloss over the differences between these viewpoints—the processes involved and the expected outcomes of each are fundamentally different. For example, if one views transformation as individuation, the outcome is self-knowledge and a more individuated personality. But each of these ways of understanding transformation can be descriptive of the experiences of different individuals or even of the same individual on different occasions.

Transformative learning theory is not only a theory in progress in terms of how people are thinking about and elaborating on it. It is also a theory in progress in relation to the expanding body of research that is supporting and asking questions of the theoretical developments. Much of the research supports Mezirow's understanding of transformation, but that may be in part because the reviews we rely on to make sense out of the field emphasize studies that are based on this approach. Research that includes spirituality, relational knowing, and authenticity are beginning to help us grasp how the various perspectives complement and elaborate on each other. Perhaps most important, the individuals who are involved in the continued development of transformative learning theory (see, for example, Wiessner, 2004) are engaged in intentional efforts to expand our thinking.

4

Transformation

The Learner's Story

In this chapter, I examine the process of transformative learning from the learner's point of view. Given that there are probably as many different transformative learning stories as there are people who experience transformation, we could just stop here. But the goal of theory development is to search for explanations and descriptions of a collection of seemingly diverse events. Based on theory development and research to date, and my own practice in which I both teach about and help foster transformative learning, I think I can present some ways in which people experience transformative learning from their perspective.

It is not just individual differences that come into play here. Transformative learning takes place in a multiplicity of contexts, it is stimulated by different types of events, and it occurs in relation to a variety of kinds of habits of minds. Studies have been conducted in higher education settings, informal learning contexts, and organizations (Taylor, 2000a, 2000b). The transformative process can be provoked by a single dramatic event, a series of almost unnoticed cumulative events, a deliberate conscious effort to make change in one's life, or by the natural developmental progression of becoming more mature. Transformative learning can have to do with a person's personal or professional life—the process I went through when my partner died was very different from how I undergo a change in perspective related to my teaching or writing.

Whether the habits of mind under revision are psychological, sociolinguistic, epistemic, moral-ethical, philosophical, or aesthetic may well determine how the learning is felt and experienced, though I am not aware of any research or even any speculation about this.

Since it is not just one story, but since I also believe there are helpful patterns to be understood, I explore the learner's transformative learning process from two dimensions in this chapter. First, I consider the process from the dimension of ways of knowing—the critical reflection perspectives and the extrarational perspectives. Since we know more about the rational approach to transformative learning from the research at this point, it was possible to give a more detailed description in this section. Second, I consider the temporal frames in which these ways of knowing may occur—epochal, incremental, and developmental. In the end, all of these views are deeply intertwined.

Ways of Knowing: The Critical Self-Reflection Perspective

Mezirow (1991, 2000) describes transformative learning in terms of phases in which critical reflection and critical self-reflection and discourse play central roles (see Chapter Two). Similarly, Brookfield (1991) describes five phases of critical thinking:

- An unexpected event leads to discomfort or perplexity.

- Appraisal or self-examination follows in which the event is identified and clarified.

- During an exploratory phase, the person tries to explain discrepancies found in the appraisal phase and investigates new ways of thinking or behaving.

- The person develops alternative perspectives in order to try out the new ways of thinking or acting.

- If the previous phase leads to new perspectives, the individual then integrates the new ways of seeing things into his or her life.

Most writers are careful to say that the models of the transformative learning process based on phases are not intended to imply that the phases are linear, discrete, or independent. That is, a person may cycle through some phases more than once, may skip some steps, or may experience different aspects of the process in varying orders. However, the very nature of the models does imply some order and some linearity. You can only reintegrate at the end, and you can only be disoriented at the beginning.

There is a good body of research to support this perspective, especially, naturally enough, among researchers who use Mezirow's writing as their theoretical framework. For example, E. Taylor (2000a, 2000b) reports that the phases of transformation are generally confirmed by some studies, even though there may not always be data related to each phase. Dewane's research (1993, cited in Taylor, 2000a) does support the existence of the phases, but not that they are sequential or that one step needs to be complete before another begins.

Let us follow this through from the point of view of the learner experiencing transformation. I generally stay with Mezirow's phases, but shorten and adapt them somewhat based on my own thinking about the process and my observations of and conversations with students.

Empowerment

Learner empowerment is both a goal of and a condition for transformative learning. An empowered learner is able to fully and freely engage in critical reflection, participate in discourse, and act on revised perspectives. A person who is oppressed, in need of shelter or food, depressed, or feeling trapped in his or her circumstances may not be able to respond to events in a potentially transformative way.

Yet unbearable social conditions can also provoke transformative learning (see, for example, Wiessner, 2000), and Frankl (1984) shows us we can achieve transformation under any conditions. It is this paradox that leads some writers to argue that changes in social conditions must precede individual transformation.

David was a student in an introductory undergraduate adult education course I was facilitating. He was in his mid or late fifties at the time I knew him, a slight, gentle man, with a hesitant way of speaking and an obviously shy nature. He mostly sat in class with his baseball cap pulled down low over his eyes, watching others carefully out from under the bill of the cap. I later learned that David was registered as a special student—he had not yet been admitted to the program—but at the time, I didn't realize this. David believed that he would be able to transfer credit from the courses he took as a special student to the degree program once he was admitted. He had been told (which, again, I only learned later) that he needed to maintain grades of B or higher to be accepted into the program.

David had a varied and colorful background. While he was in the course with me, he was driving a truck on a night shift to pay for his tuition and his living expenses. He dreamed of becoming an educator. David's writing was always refreshing and innovative in style and content, but he participated little in class.

I am not sure how many courses he took before he was told he could not come into the program, but I think it was at least five or six. He had taken two with me, but he fared less well in other courses, and he never had the courage to ask how he could improve his marks or to question his probationary position in the program. It was a financial struggle for him to pay his tuition and buy his books; in the end, all was lost.

David quietly left, refusing my and others' offers to help or to see what could be done. He felt completely powerless in the face of this academic world and its unfathomable policies and procedures. I do not know where David is now, but I think of him often. If someone, including me, had been able to discover what was going on a bit earlier and had helped empower him, I suspect his story would have turned out differently.

Disorienting Event

The literature contains some descriptions of the types of activities and approaches that educators might use in order to stimulate critical reflection (Brookfield, 1995; Gozawa, 2003; Taylor, 2000a, 2000b). I discuss these in Chapter Seven. Even when an educator deliberately sets up circumstances to promote critical reflection, not everyone or perhaps not anyone will be affected by it. Outside of the classroom context, critical reflection can be stimulated by any encounter with an unexpected or contradictory point of view. It can come through a book, a discussion with a friend, an unusual or tragic event, a change in work context, or a sudden insight.

I met Sheila when I was working in a management development program for a federal government department. My role was to help people interpret the results of a performance appraisal, which included staff, supervisor, and self-ratings, then to help the individual set up a plan for professional development. Sheila had prided herself on being task-oriented, running a tight ship, and getting the work done. She thought she had collegial (if distant) relationships with her staff. She did not socialize with her staff, nor did she want to. Sheila's self-evaluation was good, as was her supervisor's evaluation of her management skills. However, her staff ratings were in the lowest range possible and their open-ended comments indicated that they found Sheila to be arrogant, uncaring, unsupportive, and uninterested in their work or them as people. Sheila was so devastated by these unexpected results that she thought seriously about leaving her position. She had encountered perceptions of her performance at work that were completely at odds with how she saw herself.

I worked with Sheila to help her set a series of goals, strategies for meeting them, and ways to get ongoing feedback from her staff. When I heard a year or so later that she had transferred to another government office, I assumed that the appraisal process had left her feeling there was nothing she could do. I found out, though, that Sheila had indeed transformed her perspective on the manager's role and had made profound changes in her practice even though this had to be, for her, in a new location. Her personal confidence carried her through once the initial shock of the unexpected feedback abated, and she was able to examine and question her practice in a careful and productive way. I do not know for sure, but I assume that Sheila's learning was more incremental than epochal, even though the event that precipitated it was completely unexpected.

Events that stimulate critical reflection can take many forms. Being confronted with knowledge that directly contradicts previous accepted knowledge, particularly knowledge acquired from an authority figure, leads us to question what we thought we knew. We tend to accept, without question, knowledge acquired from teachers, doctors, writers, religious authorities, and, though less so these days, political leaders. When Louis Pasteur presented evidence that disease was carried by microorganisms, the medical profession had to deal first with the contradictory knowledge (reluctantly and with hostility), then examine related assumptions and their perspective on practice.

Exposure to social norms other than those to which we ascribe can also be a disorienting event. Social norms and expectations are often so deeply embedded we are not even aware of their presence. When I ask my students to evaluate their learning and select a grade that represents that evaluation, this often contradicts their prior educational experiences and their notion of the roles of teacher and learner. They may say they cannot do it, they had never imagined such a thing, and surely such a practice destroys academic standards and the quality of the entire educational system. They simply had never thought of the possibility of their being able to judge their own learning.

Larger societal and political events may provoke critical reflection for some individuals. The events of September 11, 2001, the

U.S. war on Iraq, and the tragic circumstances in the Sudan are just a few examples of situations that have led people to engage in critical reflection on their beliefs, values, and perceptions of government leaders.

Life crises—a loved one dying, a marriage breaking up, the loss of a job, financial ruin—or positive changes such as a promotion, retirement, or the completion of a years-long project can challenge individuals to reconsider their values, expectations, moral position, or self-concept. Sometimes, when I see graduate students delaying completion of a thesis, I suspect they are unconsciously avoiding the change in lifestyle that will take place once that life-consuming task is done. Traumatic crises may not lead to critical self-reflection if the person feels disempowered by the event, or it just may take some time for reflection to be possible. When my partner died, I grieved deeply. But it seemed I did not question my values or my way of seeing the world; I sensed no transformation. When a year later, nearly to the day, my favorite dog of thirteen years died, I do not think I even cried. I went to work that day. When three months after that, a second dog died, my world crashed in around me, and I questioned everything that had been holding me together—my purpose in life, the role of my friends, my work, the way I had chosen to live. Sometimes it is the building of events, one upon the other, rather than one specific event that leads to the questioning of one's perspectives.

Questioning Assumptions and Perspectives

At the heart of Mezirow's (2000, 2003a, 2003b) theory of transformative learning is critical reflection and critical self-reflection or, to use a different phrase, questioning assumptions and perspectives. People become aware of assumptions, make them explicit, consider the sources of the assumptions and the consequences of holding them, and question their validity. As I describe in Chapter Two, this also can be framed by reflection on content, process, and premise.

Becoming aware of assumptions or the habits of mind that consist of a web of related assumptions is difficult. These things are a part of the fabric of who we are. We act on them without thought. Even when we suspect that something might be wrong with how we see ourselves or the world around us, it is hard to admit that, let alone bring it out into the open and turn it around and look at it from different angles. I think of J. Clark (2005), who suggests transformative learning cannot occur without friendship—probably we most often turn to people close to us to work through the questioning of our assumptions, values, and perspectives. When I finally realized the cumulative effect of the series of deaths on my life, I simultaneously wanted to talk to and avoid my friends. I knew I needed help in questioning, but I did not want to do it.

A good educator, community developer, counselor, therapist, or other helping professional can listen and then ask the kinds of questions that help an individual critically reflect on his or her habits of mind. I discuss this more fully in Chapter Seven.

It is almost a decade now since John was my colleague, but I still think of him and pay attention when I hear he has moved from one place to another. I am not sure whether I would have called him a friend, but John and I talked rather more often and on a different level than was typical for either of us with other colleagues. He made fun of my teaching style—all that soft, facilitative stuff from adult education—and he spoke loudly and clearly about his own views of teaching. "I am a professor, therefore I profess. I am an expert, therefore my job is to share my expertise," he would say. I knew, though, that he was an anxious, overprepared teacher and that he was so exhausted after a three-hour class that he sometimes collapsed on the floor of his office. It was impossible, it seemed, for John to acknowledge even the smallest gap in his expertise, one that would allow him to question his assumptions about teaching. I did not want or expect John to adopt my teaching style, but it was clear he was unhappy at some level with his own. We talked often and used humor in order to be able to speak safely about our differences.

I left that university, and John moved on to another university. To my surprise, about a year later, he invited me to give a workshop on fostering critical reflection for the faculty at his new location. When I was there and having dinner with him and his wife, he revealed that he had indeed been questioning his beliefs about teaching during the time we talked and in the year since. He had also talked to other people, done some reading, and had made important changes in his views. He still subscribed to a teacher-centered model, but he experienced a deep shift in how he saw himself as a person and a teacher.

Sheared, in a symposium (Brookfield, Sheared, Johnson-Bailey, and Colin, 2005) at the Adult Education Research Conference, describes growing up as a female African American child in the South. "At the time," she says, "I did not understand I was living at the margins" (p. 480), but later in life, she comes to understand how "race in particular affects how others view you and the impact that this interpretation might have on how we view ourselves" (p. 480). This understanding generalized to Sheared's interpretation of the literature and the media.

Discourse, Dialogue, and Support

As I discuss in Chapter Two, and as I mention repeatedly throughout this section, discourse, dialogue, and support from others appear to play a major role in transformative learning. Mezirow (2003a) defines discourse as "dialogue involving the assessment of beliefs, feelings, and values" (p. 59). He sees creating the conditions for transformative learning, including critical reflection and discourse, as being the essence of adult education and the defining characteristic of the role of the adult educator. Brookfield (1991) suggests that we need others to help us break out of our frameworks of interpretation. Other people reflect our point of view back to us and act as a mirror from a different vantage point.

There are varied roles that others (educators, peers, friends, colleagues) play in transformative learning. Most obviously, perhaps, people play a role in questioning and challenging, as Brookfield suggests, helping us unearth our hidden assumptions and question their validity. A friend may ask a friend, "Is it really necessary for you to talk to your adult son daily on the telephone?" thereby encouraging her to notice a potentially overly dependent relationship. An educator may ask students to write a letter or participate in a debate from a point of view opposite their own, thus promoting awareness of their reasons for holding that view. Others can assist us in not only articulating our own perspective but also in seeing alternatives.

Dialogue and support play a vital role in helping individuals maintain a good sense of self during a time that they may be making unsettling changes in the way they see themselves. This may involve general support of the "you are OK" variety, but it may also be specific feedback on changes that a learner is considering or in the process of making. Educators especially need to be aware of learners' needs for supportive and challenging feedback during transformative learning. Mezirow (1991) says that it is unethical to engage in transformative learning if we are unwilling to support learners as they go through it.

There are so many learners' stories that could be told here. I think of Angela, who, on the last day of a five-day workshop on transformative learning, offered to make a presentation about her father's death, which had occurred several years earlier. Using photos and collages, she cried as she told her story for the very first time to this supportive group—she had been unable to speak of it before. I think of Lois, an independent and articulate woman who managed a large household, full-time studies, and part-time work and was terrified to the point of paralysis at the notion of making a presentation to her peers. With the help of dialogue, rehearsal, and feedback, she managed to overcome that fear and speak about a work of art she had created. And I think of Yeshey who was chosen by her home government in Bhutan to come to Canada to learn about alternative perspectives on education. Yeshey relies on the support of her fellow Bhutanese students in this strange country, and she has gradually formed alliances with Canadian educators.

Ways of Knowing: The Extrarational Perspective

Whether it is expressed as despair or joy, conflict or harmony, or anger or delight, dramatic opportunities for transformative learning exist when we are able to engage imaginatively with life's events (Dirkx, 2001a). Dirkx relays several anecdotes to illustrate what he means—a frustrated GED student who would rather be doing pottery than studying math, an individual whose readings on adult development theory illuminated her own life, a community college instructor who was resigned to not having time for collaborative work. In his story of Clara, Dirkx (1997) describes an emotional outburst from a student who reacted strongly to the group work taking place in a class. Feeling stunned and betrayed, Dirkx was unable to pick up on this moment, and the class "limped along emotionally deflated and anemic for the remainder of the term" (p. 81). It is by paying attention to these moments that transformative learning can be fostered through soul work, imagination, and emotions. Dirkx advocates the use of journal writing, artistic projects, novels, and poetry—essentially any strategy that connects learners to soul work, which he describes as critical to personal transformation (Dirkx, 2001b).

Our classrooms and workshop venues are not typically places where we encourage or even allow emotions, imagination, and fantasy. It is a common habit of mind to view educational contexts as places for the presentation of information and serious, rational discussion. We avoid or smooth over conflict, we bring things "back on track" when someone becomes fanciful. As Dirkx (1997) says, we are products of a culture that devalues matters of soul. When I first encountered Dirkx's work, I needed to examine my discomfort. As a young student, I never had the courage to speak at all in a class, never mind to express emotion or display imagination, and throughout my teaching career, being quiet, reflective, and analytical has been natural for me. Yet I am drawn to matters of the soul and am now convinced of the importance of working with images and feelings in fostering transformative learning. I have long encouraged journal writing, and in recent years I have also encouraged artistic projects of all kinds, and incorporated movies, music, and fiction into my classes. There is no doubt that these activities are transformative for many students. What I still struggle with is letting the moment be when there is anger, fear, conflict, or despair—"facilitating transformative learning in which emotional reactions to the text are regarded as imagistic manifestations of inner selves" (Dirkx, 2001a, p. 15).

How does this look and feel from the learners' perspective? Feller, Jensen, Marie, and others (2004) describe the experiences of Cohort 14, in which transformative learning was regarded as a practice of wholeness—a balance of mind, body, spirit, and emotion. Among a wide range of diverse experiences, participants kept journals, learned through the body by going for walks or meditating, engaged in spiritual activities such as lighting a candle and visualizing members of the group, and practiced specialized forms of dialogue designed to foster sharing and trust. Unfortunately, aside from telling us what they did and integrating this into a quadrinity model, the authors do not describe how they experienced transformative learning.

Although she was focusing on spirituality among women adult educators engaged in promoting social change, Tisdell (2000b) also noted that spirituality was a part of her participants' personal transformation. Tisdell's research participants saw spirituality as not being about rationality, but rather about the wholeness of all creation and making meaning out of life purpose. Experiences were in the "realm of mystery" (p. 331) and symbolic processes.

Sawyer (2003) tells the story of Dr. Bruce Lipton, a cellular biologist who experienced a deep paradigm shift from a reductionist, determinist worldview to an understanding based on quantum physics, one founded on holism and uncertainty. For Lipton, this was an uninvited conversion from a nonspiritual to a fully spiritual person. He felt "overwhelmed with joy and exhilaration" (p. 372) and felt compelled to share his discovery with others at 2:15 A.M.

Kasl and Elias (2000), in their description of transformative learning as the "expansion of consciousness in any human system . . .[,] the collective as well as individual" through "appreciatively accessing and receiving the symbolic contents of the unconscious" (p. 233), illustrate their perspective with the experience of belonging to the Transformative Learning Collaborative. From their two different perspectives, Kasl and Elias both see the group itself as moving to a more inclusive, differentiated, permeable, and integrated perspective.

I remember Jim from three or four summers ago. He was probably the oldest person in the group of students taking an adult education methods course, and he obviously had a long-held fear of being "in school." For the first week and a half, Jim was the class clown. He was friendly and funny; he found a joke in everything we did. We all liked Jim very much, but I was also uncomfortable with how Jim used his clown role to avoid anything that might get serious. I no longer remember the exact circumstances that led to Jim's dramatic moment, but it was one of those everyday occurrences to which Dirkx (2000) suggests we pay attention. Jim suddenly shouted out, "I can't do this, I can't be a teacher, this was not meant to be, I am quitting now!" We were stunned. I thought, "What did I say? What did I do?" and I could see the same questions in others' faces. It was a beautiful summer day. The sun was shining into our classroom windows, and someone was going by with a lawnmower. The only thing I could think to do was to break and somehow acknowledge Jim's moment. I suggested that we walk in the nearby woods and just ponder what we were all doing here. I knew Jim was not connected to me; he was much more comfortable with the presence of men. As we were leaving the classroom, I quietly asked two or three of the men in the group to walk with Jim.

We wandered for half an hour or so. I did not speak to Jim. I sensed I should not. But I participated by walking and pondering with others. After class, a group of the men took Jim to play miniature golf, then to a local pub for a meal, then back to the residence for an evening of talk. The next day, Jim came to me and said that he thought "it would be OK," that he could do it after all. He dropped the clown role. He participated in serious dialogue, he became open about his fears, and he confessed to me that he was terrified of writing anything. I think this was an extrarational transformative experience.

Many of my students have experienced transformative learning through artistic learning projects. I have seen innumerable wonderful creations and listened to the stories accompanying them. It is hard to choose which story to tell, but Lisa's experience stands out for me. In a week-long workshop on transformative learning, Lisa decided to create a collage to represent her transformative experiences. Lisa is a music teacher, but she had never worked with the visual arts. She described how she set up a space in her New York apartment for her work and how she looked forward to working on the project each day. "The time flew," she said, "the hours disappeared when I worked on the collage." After the week's end, Lisa sent me digital photos of her collage, and we discussed her use of color, the images and symbols she included, and the meaning of the work for her. It was about two months later when I received a long and enthusiastic e-mail from Lisa. She had a new CD coming out, and when asked about the cover of the CD, she immediately thought of her collage. The collage would become the CD cover. But more than that, Lisa wrote about the depth of her experience in creating the collage, how she saw herself in a different way and changed her perspective on the meaning of art and music and the connection between the two.

When I think about the numerous sculptures, paintings, poems, short stories, music CDs, quilts, stained glass works, kaleidoscopes, and collages that I have been honored to see in my practice, I am struck by the transformative learning process inherent in these projects. It certainly does not involve a reasoned, critically reflective progression. The transformative experience may be a flash of insight, a profoundly moving moment in which a person's view of himself or herself and the world is changed, or it may be a slow unfolding of the creative process revealed nonverbally and moving from tacit to explicit. In all of her writing, Greene (1995) eloquently invites educators to restructure and enhance learning experiences through the imagination and the arts.

The Temporal Dimension: Incremental or Epochal

Mezirow (2000) distinguishes between transformative learning that occurs gradually over time (incremental) and that which is a sudden and dramatic change in perspective (epochal). E. Taylor (1997) found evidence of this distinction in a critical review of doctoral dissertations on transformative learning. Incremental transformation creeps up on a person over months or even years, perhaps partly or mostly an unconscious process, until the day when he or she looks back and says, "I was a different person then." From the transformative stories I hear in my practice and from my own experience, it seems that transformative learning is more often incremental than epochal. Research that describes transformative processes usually focuses on some defined period of time, such as a three-week residential program (for example, Cohen, 2004) or a three-year slice of people's professional lives (for example, Cranton and Carusetta, 2004a). Such research examines transformation during that time, so it does not ask about gradual and dramatic changes in perspective. In E. Taylor's (2000a, 2000b) review of the research on transformative learning, he suggests that even "trigger events" or "initial reactions" extend over a period of time rather than being dramatic moments.

Since it is Mezirow who proposes that there are both epochal and incremental transformative experiences, and since it is also Mezirow who approaches transformative learning theory from a critically reflective, problem-solving perspective, we can only assume that even the epochal experience is not one of sudden illumination, the light bulb appearing over the person's head. Even if the precipitating event is abrupt, it seems to be followed by a process of unfolding, including critical reflection, discourse, and a conscious revision of assumptions.

It seems that there are several possibilities here. There could be

- A traumatic event that initiates a careful, reasoned exploration of values and beliefs and leads to a changed perspective

- A traumatic event that lies dormant for a long period and only gradually leads a person to change

- A deeply-felt, positive experience or a series of positive experiences that leads to a questioning of either personal habits of mind or perspectives on the world

- A sudden, disturbing experience that leads to an immediate and nonrational switch in beliefs

- A gradual, unnoticed, and perhaps not entirely conscious process of change over time that is only recognized in retrospect

- A series of small life changes, none of which are dramatic in themselves, but that lead cumulatively to a revision in a habit of mind over time

- A deliberate, conscious effort over time to change oneself and the way one sees the world

Whether we choose to label all of these as transformative learning would depend on our theoretical perspective.

In Anna Quindlen's (2002) novel, *Blessings*, Skip has just been released from jail, where he was serving time for robbery. Skip has deeply embedded assumptions about himself and others—you just do not get out of the life you were born into. He sees this in the stories of his peers and people in the small community where he lives. People do not move from being trash to being upstanding citizens, from poverty to wealth, from unemployment to respectable work. When a days-old infant is left on Skip's doorstep, he knows this was meant to be. This baby is his to care for. He learns the practical things he needs to know, he buys a book on baby care, he goes to a Wal-Mart in a nearby town (where he will not be recognized) to buy the things a baby needs. Initially, it is a matter of sheer survival. Skip does not think about why he is doing what he is doing. He suffers through the sleepless nights, manages to hide the baby as he is working as a caretaker, avoids his former pub mates, and in spite of his exhaustion and fear, delights in her first smile and the way she holds his finger. Skip finds support in unlikely places—his tough, dictatorial, over-eighty employer and the daughter of his employer's maid. He dreams of a future where the baby grows up and goes to school, where he has a house and perhaps a small business. And then he begins to see that a person can get out of the life he was seemingly born into. If there is a reason for doing it, and the baby is a reason, a person can change. Skip's worldview is transformed. Even though misunderstanding and tragedy visit him again, Skip sees himself and the world around him in a new way.

In the summer program in which I facilitate the journey of trades and technical people into the world of teaching, there usually are no disturbing events in people's lives, even though the move from practicing a trade to becoming a teacher of that trade could be described as a major life transition. But there are no babies left on doorsteps. Everyone has deliberately chosen to enter the teaching profession after thought, reflection, and discussion. My course is one of several courses for a mandatory (if they wish to teach in the community college system) Certificate in Adult Education, and it is the second and last summer course. For many of the participants, the program and perhaps this last summer course is a transformative experience; I hear their stories and read their journals every year, and people often keep in touch with me and their classmates long after the program's end. Research shows, too, that many of the students engaging in this transition see it as transformative (Sokol and Cranton, 1998).

We are together six hours a day for three weeks. Participants choose the topics they wish to explore; I provide the readings and design most of the learning activities (usually in the last week, the students lead several of the learning activities). There most often is no sudden and dramatic change, but there is, one after another, day by day, a series of different points of view, questions, challenges to perceptions of what teaching means, sharing of experiences, and dialogue about educational practice. It is when people are nearing the end of the program and sometimes after they have returned to their colleges that they see and are able to describe their experience as transformative. To me, this is incremental transformation.

The Temporal Dimension: Developmental Transformation

From the developmental perspective, transformative learning takes place through the negotiation of developmental transitions (Daloz, 1999). Daloz sees this process as intuitive, holistic, and contextually based. It is a journey influenced by social environment, community, and family. Tennant (1993) proposes that transformative learning occurs along with or as a part of normal life transitions. Most adult development models (for example, King and Kitchener, 1994) describe stages of development in which people move from black-and-white, authority-based thinking through to complex, integrative web-like thinking in which there is no objective truth outside of the self. In his constructive-developmental approach to transformative learning, Kegan (2000) proposes five increasingly complex epistemologies, which begin with perceptions, move through to abstractions (the socialized mind) and abstract systems (the self-authoring mind) to the dialectical (the self-transforming mind). In the most complex epistemology, people create a distance from their own internal theories and perspectives so that they can recognize their incompleteness and embrace contradictory systems simultaneously. Kegan's approach does not depend on initiating or trigger events, although he does suggest that the modern social world demands increasingly complex ways of making meaning out of experience.

Based on the literature and extensive consultation with adult educators, K. Taylor (2000) describes dimensions of development from the learners' perspective. She organizes thirty-six characteristics into five dimensions: (1) Toward Knowing as a Dialogical Process (inquiring into and responding to others' ideas, pursuing the possibility of objective truth); (2) Toward a Dialogical Relationship to Oneself (exploring experience through a framework of analysis, making meaning of life stories within contexts); (3) Toward Being a Continuous Learner (challenging oneself to learn in new realms, drawing on multiple capacities for learning); (4) Toward Self-Agency and Self-Authorship (accepting responsibility for choices, distinguishing what one has created for oneself from what is imposed by social forces); and (5) Toward Connection with Others (experiencing oneself as a part of something larger, contributing to a collective endeavour).

In her research, Berger (2004) explores, from a developmental perspective, how people feel when they are on the threshold of transformation, or on the "growing edge" as she puts it. In a reanalysis of data from twenty interviews, Berger looked for places where participants seemed to be on the edge of their knowing. She wanted to understand how that point where the old perspective is given up and the new perspective not quite formed was experienced. This interesting approach yielded variable results—for some people the edge was frightening and unpleasant, for others it felt exciting and energizing. Some participants appreciated being able to "dance on the edge of their knowing" (p. 343), and others felt reluctantly dragged along. Many people had difficulty articulating how they felt—language failed.

Belenky, Bond, and Weinstock (1997) bring a different perspective to developmental transformation. In a study of four community groups, the leaders held a passionate belief in people's ability to lead themselves and therefore saw their role as one of midwife-leaders "drawing out" others. The organizations called on the traditional gender roles of supporting the development of others through connected knowing.

I notice it more as I grow older, but I think adults of any age who look back and consider how they thought or felt about their experiences ten years previously usually recognize noticeable differences in how they process things and that this processing becomes increasingly complex. When we talk about wisdom, we associate this with age and maturity. By wisdom, we mean, at least in part, the intricacy or sophistication of a person's perspectives on life. There is, as Kegan (2000) emphasizes, not just a change, but a change in form and structure.

Summary

It has been an interesting experience for me, in writing this chapter, to read descriptions of how learners perceive transformative learning in the literature, remember and attempt to articulate the experiences of students in my classes, and push myself into considering transformative experience from the inside by using perspectives alternative to the familiar and comfortable (for me) cognitive perspective.

We know quite a lot about what transformation looks like from the learner's perspective when we view the process as one with critical self-reflection and discourse at its center. More research has examined this way of understanding transformative learning than others. In this chapter, I discuss what disorienting events, questioning of assumptions and perspectives, and discourse, dialogue, and support look like from the point of view of the person engaged in those processes.

With the help of Dirkx's writing (2000, 2001a, 2001b) and the experiences of students I have worked with, I explore extrarational transformative learning from the learner's perspective. The joy, fear, exhilaration, and the wholeness of the intersection of mind, body, and spirit come through in people's descriptions, though in many ways, it is beyond language and difficult to capture in a linear strings of words. I hope I have managed to portray something of how people feel when they work outside of the realm of cognitive rationality and find deep, powerful shifts in the way they see themselves and the world.

Both rational and extrarational transformation can occur suddenly and dramatically, gradually over time, or as a developmental process. The research tends to reveal primarily gradual, incremental experiences, though the appeal of the "burning bush" phenomenon is strong. When we tell stories about transformative experiences, it is more appealing to emphasize the dramatic (for example, Sawyer's [2003] story of Dr. Lipton's transformation). In the end, however, it seems that from the perspective of the person experiencing transformation, it is more often a gradual accumulation of ordinary experiences that leads to a deep shift in thinking, a shift that may only become clear when it is over.

From the developmental perspective, Daloz (1999) helps us see transformation as the negotiation of developmental transitions—an intuitive, holistic, and contextually based process—the movement from one stage or phase of development to another. The developmental theorists all describe, in one form or another, the movement from simple to increasingly complex ways of seeing the world. To use Mezirow's language, as people transform habits of mind, they acquire perspectives that are more open, permeable, and better justified. I especially appreciated Berger's (2004) exploration of what it felt like to be on the edge, in the transition, and between the perspectives.

E. Taylor (2000a, 2003b) points out the need for more longitudinal studies of transformative learning and studies in which the researcher is present during the experience. We need, he suggests, data from both the perspective of the participant and the researcher; collaborative inquiry is a promising approach here. After searching for ways to represent transformative learning from the learner's perspective, I would like to echo Taylor's suggestions.

5

Individual Differences

Following the thinking of Mezirow (2000), Kegan (2000), and others, transformative learning theory is based on a constructivist view of the world. Some of the assumptions underlying constructivism are that people participate in the construction of reality, and this construction occurs within a context that influences it; commonly accepted views are socially constructed; understanding depends on a social process; people can attend to complex communications and organize complexity; and human interactions are based on social roles with implicit rules. In other words, we see the world through a lens constructed in our interaction with our social context. We also make decisions related to our perceptions in our own way. We are individuals living in and influenced by our social world, and we are individuals with important differences among us in the way we live, learn, work, and develop.

The adult education literature contains many ways of classifying and explaining individual differences. Developmental phase, learning style, multiple intelligences, personality type, cognitive style, past experience, and self-directed learning readiness are just some of the ways in which writers try to account for learners' behavior and to predict how they will behave in the future. Many of these attempts to classify learners lead to dichotomies or mutually exclusive categories. People are described as visual learners or auditory learners; they are in the leaving-home phase or the moving-into-the-adult-world phase.

There is value in this; we need patterns and commonalities and trends in order to make sense of things. However, we could also overlook the diversity and complexity of human learning if we are too rigid in our classifying schemes.

Psychological type theory (Jung, [1921] 1971) is a meaningful way of understanding individual differences without oversimplification. Unfortunately, many of the inventories based on Jung's work do stereotype, but Jung accepts that individuals construe their own meaning of the world, and, at the same time, he attempts to classify these differences without losing their complexity.

In this chapter, I view the process of transformative learning through the lens of psychological type theory. I first describe Jung's theory, then go through the various aspects of transformation to see how they might be different for people with different psychological preferences. I do not wish to minimize or ignore the important differences in how Jung and Mezirow think about the human psyche. I respect Dirkx's (see Cranton and Dirkx, 2005) uneasiness about grafting psychological type theory onto Mezirow's transformative learning theory. Jung's work on individuation and other psychological processes is extrarational in nature. However, his writing on psychological type theory can stand alone, I believe, and can be used as a way of deepening our understanding of transformative learning.

Psychological Type Theory

The ideal and aim of science do not consist in giving the most exact description of the facts . . . but in establishing certain laws, which are merely abbreviated expressions for many diverse processes that are yet to be conceived to be somehow correlated. This aim goes beyond the purely empirical by means of the *concept*, which, though it may have general and proved validity, will always be a product of the subjective constellation of the investigator. . . . This well-known fact must

nowhere be taken more seriously than in psychology.
(Jung,[1921]1971, pp. 8–9)

Jung argues that the observer in psychology must see both subjec-
tively and objectively; he is highly critical of the idea that there can
be objective psychology. Following constructivist thinking, Jung real-
izes that the theorist who attempts to explain patterns in others is
doing so through his or her own perspective. He comments frequently and powerfully on the difficulty in describing and interpreting psychological types. He repeatedly cautions his readers against
stereotyping and makes a strong case against the quantification or
measurement of psychological type preferences (since this runs the
risk of objectifying the observation). Today there is an abundance of
such measurements, and I believe it is possible to maintain the integrity of Jung's work by using profiles rather than categories and taking great care with the language of interpretation (for example, see
Cranton and Knoop, 1995). Jung also is clear about psychological
type being but one way of discussing human characteristics.

Introversion and Extraversion

Jung ([1921] 1971) began the development of psychological type
theory by recognizing introverted and extraverted attitudes. No
one is entirely introverted or extraverted; these preferences are on a
continuum.

   Introversion is an inner orientation. The subject, the self, is
more important than the object, the world outside of the self. A person with a tendency toward introversion views the world subjec-
tively, in relation to himself or herself. In everyday language, we
associate introversion with being quiet and shy, and this may be
so, but it is not necessarily a characteristic of introversion. The distinguishing factor is the orientation to the self rather than to the
outside world. When it is raining, the person who is more introverted interprets the rain in relation to how he or she feels about it:
"It is raining, and I feel depressed when it rains," or "This scene

reminds me of the time when I experienced one of the happiest occasions of my life." Responses to others, to events, and to readings are personalized, related to the self.

Extraversion is an outward orientation. When demonstrating an extraverted attitude, a person thinks, feels, and acts in relation to the object, to the things in the world. Objects, people, and events in the world are accepted rather than interpreted in relation to the self. Jung describes it as a "ready acceptance of external happenings, a desire to influence and be influenced by events, a need to join in and get 'with it,' the capacity to endure bustle and noise of every kind, and actually find them enjoyable, constant attention to the surrounding world, the cultivation of friends and acquaintances. . ." (p. 549). Jung goes on in this description to say that people who are more extraverted are not very discriminating in their selection of acquaintances, are overly interested in how they present themselves, and have "a strong tendency to make a show of" themselves. I find it interesting to notice how Jung's language borders on reflecting distaste for extraversion; Jung was clearly on the introverted end of this continuum himself. The dialogue below indicates how a person with more extraversion and a person with more introversion may vary in their response to information. The extraverted attitude focuses on the external world as it is, and the more introverted attitude personalizes the information.

Illustration of Introversion and Extraversion

Sam: My uncle turned 101 last week!

Pamela (more extraverted): How wonderful! How is his health? Does he still live on his own?

Arthur (more introverted): I'll never live so long. The way I live, I'll be lucky to see sixty-five.

Jung emphasized the importance of integrating the introverted and extraverted attitudes. Writing in the 1920s, he argued against the church and modern science, both of which he saw as denying the reality of the inner world at the expense of objective, empirically determined descriptions. One of his missions was to establish the validity of the internal experiences of ideas, fantasy, and archetypes, which he saw as necessary for individuation and self-actualization. It is interesting to think about this in relation to the movement to bring the extrarational into transformative learning (see Chapter Three). Jung was making the same argument more than eighty years ago.

Functions

Jung was not satisfied with introversion and extraversion as a way of describing differences among people. It did not account well enough for the differences he observed. It took him another ten years to formulate the now very familiar four psychological functions: thinking, feeling, sensing, and intuition.

Thinking and feeling became, in the final form of the theory, the two judgmental (or rational) functions. Use of the thinking function involves making judgments and decisions through logical analysis and problem solving. Use of the feeling function involves making judgments and decisions by the considering of values, one's own values and those of others.

Sensing and intuition are the two perceptive (or irrational) functions. Using the sensing function to perceive relies on gathering information through the senses—sight, touch, hearing, taste. Using the intuitive function to perceive relies on hunches, imagination, and fantasy; the perception occurs in an unconscious way. "The content presents itself whole and complete, without our being able to explain or discover how this content came into existence," says Jung ([1921] 1971, p. 453).

Psychological Types

The combination of the two attitudes (introversion and extraversion) and the four functions (thinking, feeling, sensing, and intuition) yield eight psychological types. Some popular inventories, such as the Myers-Briggs Type Indicator (MBTI), come up with different combinations (sixteen types for the MBTI), but here I choose to stay congruent with Jung's theory. I review each of the eight combinations of attitudes and functions with a cautionary note that no one has all of the characteristics of one type.

Extraverted Thinking. When thinking is extraverted, it focuses on the object outside of the self, the external world. Using information from the external world, a person who prefers extraverted thinking applies logical and analytical processes to solve problems and make judgments. He or she aims to establish order in life and is more interested in facts and ideas than other people. Therefore, the person may appear to be impersonal or unfriendly to others who are more people-oriented.

People who prefer extraverted thinking usually expect others around them to adhere to their principles. They may assume the role of social or organizational reformer and are generally idealists. Their thinking is positive, productive, progressive, and creative. They are sure of themselves and their ideals and principles and will pursue these ideals in the face of any opposition.

Extraverted Feeling. Feeling is also a judgmental function; however, rather than using objective criteria, people who prefer this psychological type use traditional or generally accepted values (those external to the self) to make judgments. Jung puts it well when he writes, "I may feel moved, for instance to say that something is 'beautiful' or 'good,' not because I find it 'beautiful' or 'good' from my own subjective feeling about it, but because it is fitting and politic to call it so, since a contrary judgment would upset the general feeling situation" (p. 355).

Their reliance on generally accepted values leads people who prefer extraverted feeling to a desire for harmony in their surroundings—conflicts in values would upset their process of using values to determine their behavior. As a result, they easily adapt their own stance to match that expressed by others. They smooth over differences. People with this preference make friends easily, work well with others in groups, and are very pleasant to be with.

Extraverted Sensing. When a person's sensing function is focused on the world external to the self, he or she perceives the world as it is and accumulates experiences of reality with little interpretation or judgment. People with this preference are interested in tangible reality, are practical and down-to-earth, are not bothered by violations of logic, and do not care very much about the relationships among the things they perceive or abstract and theoretical conceptualizations of the world.

Individuals who prefer extraverted sensing enjoy things of the senses—good food, beautiful objects, and attractive people. The concrete facts and experiences they perceive with their senses provide the basis of what comes next. What happens once will happen again; what worked well last time will work well next time. Others see these individuals as good company and people who enjoy life.

Extraverted Intuition. When intuition is focused outwardly, unconscious perception is directed to external objects. Jung says this is manifested by "an attitude of expectancy, by vision and penetration" (p. 366). The intuitive function transmits images, leading the person who prefers this function to seek the possibilities inherent in every situation. Ordinary events hold great potential; every locked door needs to be opened.

People who prefer extraverted intuition are intensely interested in new situations, events, and objects; they approach them without judgment. They are likely to be initiators of new enterprises, champions of causes, and visionaries. They may appear to be indifferent to anything that is not a part of their vision and uninfluenced by thoughts or feelings, their own or others'. Sometimes, when the novelty of a new project wears off, people who are strongly extraverted and intuitive may lose interest and abandon the project. Other times, they may appear manipulative as they go about reforming some aspect of the world. However, their great enthusiasm and their ability to visualize possibilities draws others to their charisma and passion for change.

Illustration of the Extraverted Functions

Situation: A work team has come to an impasse in preparing a marketing plan for electronic mosquito repellers.

Sheila (with a preference for extraverted thinking): Let's just get this done! Here, I've divided the job up into five parts. If we each take one part and bring it back tomorrow, I'll put it together.

Pat (with a preference for extraverted feeling): It's important that everyone feels involved in this decision. Let's just stop a minute and hear from each of the team members, find out what everyone would like to do.

Jim (with a preference for extraverted sensing): Why don't we just look up the marketing plan we had for the ant traps. That worked well. We can just follow that.

Robert (with a preference for extraverted intuition): Wait, wait. We need to consider the bigger picture. The environmental issues, the alternatives to electronic repellers—there's so much more to bring into this before we finalize the plan. Why, I think we could hook up with the Green Party and . . .

Introverted Thinking. When thinking is focused inwardly, the criteria used for making judgments come from within the person rather than from the external world as they do when thinking is extraverted. Ideas have their origin not in objective data, but in subjective (of the self) thought. People who prefer introverted thinking are relatively uninfluenced by the thoughts and perceptions of other people. They enjoy working with theories and models and are less interested in the practical application of these theories. They like to formulate questions, gain new insights, and create new theories, often just for the sake of creating the theory.

The strength of individuals who have a strong introverted thinking function lies in the clarity, organization, and precision of their ideas, and less so in originality or their ability to persuade others of their ideas. They may only collect facts as evidence for their views and discard those that do not fit. They have strong inner principles by which they live, they are reflective, and they value truth. People with this preference need time to think things through, as the judgmental processes are internal. To other people, those who use introverted thinking may seem inconsiderate or even arrogant, because they tend to judge others harshly when their ideas are not quickly embraced or appreciated.

Introverted Feeling. When the feeling function is inner-oriented, judgments are made based on subjective, inner values rather than the traditional, accepted values important to extraverted feeling. Values are personalized; they come from within. Jung describes people who prefer introverted feeling as "mostly silent, inaccessible, and hard to understand" (p. 389). Because of the introverted focus, others simply do not see what is going on in that person. People with a preference for introverted feeling have an outward demeanor of harmony, but they may be inclined to melancholy. They prefer to live in a quiet, inner world of their own values, visions, and feelings. They have an inner intensity that others do not see, and they may be misunderstood as a result of this.

When individuals have a strong preference for introverted feeling, the outside world only acts as a stimulus; they are not much influenced by the actions or values of others. Although they most often choose not to express it, they possess a depth of feeling others usually cannot grasp. They enjoy solitude, and have a strong self of self-containment.

Introverted Sensing. When the sensing function is introverted, it is guided by the subjective sensation in reaction to an objective stimulus. In other words, the person who prefers introverted sensing may see the same object as another person sees, but he or she sees it in a subjective way—it is personalized and special meaning is attached to it. The senses are used to gather information from the world, and that information is immediately made personal, related to the self.

An individual who prefers introverted sensing, might, for example, collect paintings and be primarily interested in how those paintings reflect various facets of himself or herself. Or, looking at an object, the person might immediately respond in terms of a memory of a similar object or a personal association with the object (that chair reminds me of the one my mother sat in when I was a child; that color is the color of the shirt I wore when I went for my first job interview). If asked to describe the object, the person would give a representation of their impression of the object. People who have a strong introverted sensing function are more in tune with their own perceptions of reality than with those of others. They prefer quiet arrangements and routines. They enjoy taking care of the details of life, and feel a sense of accomplishment when all of the little chores have been taken care of for the day. Their greatest strength is their sensitivity to people and objects, but others may see this as arbitrary and unpredictable, as it is based on interpretation rather than reality.

Introverted Intuition. People who have a preference for introverted intuition are also stimulated by an external object, but rather than attaching personal meaning to it as happens with the sensing function, the object releases inner images and fantasies. Jung sees these inner images as being released from the unconscious. This person may look at a chair and imagine dozens of different ways in which chairs could be constructed or see the possible alternative uses for chairs. The images need not have any immediate utility (others may describe this as daydreaming), and they may be fleeting.

Individuals who strongly prefer introverted intuition may be those who come up with ideas on how things could be—they have unusual and imaginative ways of seeing the world. However, they often cannot connect these ideas to reality, as their focus is inner-oriented. They may be frequently misunderstood, described as mysterious, not able to reveal themselves to others, and seen as indifferent or even untruthful (since they are not connected to tangible reality).

Illustration of the Introverted Functions

Situation: Observing a painting at the Museum of Modern Art

Patricia (with a preference for introverted thinking): I like the symmetry of the lines and the use of blue and green to develop mood. But this yellow blotch over here doesn't seem to fit.

Tony (with a preference for introverted feeling): I feel calm and happy when I look at this. The blues and greens are calming and the yellow represents happy sunshine for me.

Pamela (with a preference for introverted sensing): This really reminds me of the wallpaper that was in my parents' bedroom when I was a child. I always felt so comforted by that combination of colors.

Victor (with a preference for introverted intuition): I am reminded of the way blue symbolizes the unconscious, water, the womb, and I can see that there could be fish underneath that water, fish that are devouring each other in a battle to come to the exit from the womb.

Profiles

Now that I have taken the various facets of psychological type theory apart and described each one separately, it is important to put them back together again and understand this as an integrative, holistic way of seeing a person, not as a categorization system or a one-dimensional, stereotyping label. Even though Jung cautions against quantifying psychological type preferences (and I agree with this caution), I think we can create useful descriptions of preferences if we maintain a holistic view. A colleague and I designed and validated such an approach to assessing psychological type preferences (Cranton and Knoop, 1995; Vital Knowledge Software, 2003).

Every person has a profile of preferences. First, most people prefer introversion or extraversion, even though they have both in their personality. Second, most people have a dominant or most preferred function—this is the function they are most comfortable using and the one they use naturally and often. Third, individuals have an auxiliary or secondary function, which they use less often but are still comfortable with. Since everyone both perceives the world and makes judgments on it, the dominant and auxiliary functions cover both of these areas. For example, if thinking is my strongest preference, then I need an auxiliary function that is perceptive—either sensing or intuition. Fourth, people have an inferior function or a shadow side—the function they rarely use and do not understand. This function is mostly unconscious.

If the strength of each of the eight attitude-function combinations is assessed or described separately and then put together into a profile, a wealth of information can be obtained. Based on my experience in working with psychological type profiles, I give a few examples of the kinds of understandings we can reach:

- If a person's thinking and feeling functions are equal in strength on her extraverted side, but she has a stronger thinking function on her introverted side, she will have difficulty making judgments in the external world and will need to turn inward to use her thinking function.

- If a person's extraverted feeling function is strong and his introverted thinking function is equally strong, he will make judgments when he is inwardly oriented that do not seem to hold up when he takes them into the outside world.

- When all four judgmental functions (extraverted thinking and feeling, introverted thinking and feeling) are equally strong, the person will experience conflict and difficulty in making decisions and judgments.

- When the sensing and intuitive functions are equally strong, the person will flip back and forth between focusing on the tangible, here and now world and the possibilities for changing the world or seeing it in different ways.

- A person whose perceptive functions (sensing and intuition) are much stronger than her judgmental functions (thinking and feeling) will be reluctant to stop collecting information or envisioning possibilities and come to closure or to a decision.

There are many more combinations of preferences that could be discussed, but my goal here is to emphasize the complexity of psychological type profiles when they are viewed as a whole. Looking only at a person's dominant function or dominant and auxiliary function limits us.

Differentiation

Some people, at different points in their lives, do not express clear preferences for one function over another. Jung calls this undifferentiation. "Differentiation means the development of differences, the separation of parts from a whole. . . . So long as a function is still so fused with one or more other functions—thinking with feeling, feeling with sensation, etc.—that it is unable to operate on its own, it is an *archaic* condition, i.e. not differentiated" (Jung, [1921] 1971, p. 424). If we think of taking an average of many individuals, we could come up with an aggregate profile of preferences in which each of the functions would be of about the same strength. This would represent the collective of humanity but would tell us nothing about any individual.

Jung sees the goal of psychological development being to differentiate ourselves from the collective of humanity. How am I different? What makes me unique? Who am I really, as separate from another? When a person's psychological type profile is such that he or she has equal preferences for the functions, it is as though this is one with the collective of humanity. That person has no unique pattern. It is as though he or she is trying to be everything that everyone is, unable to say "I am like this, but I am not like that."

At the same time, Jung says that the conscious development of the psychological type functions is a lifelong goal. If a person deliberately chooses to develop other ways of being and becomes aware of and able to use different functions at different times, this is working toward a kind of wholeness, integration with humanity. The key here is consciousness. Unconscious undifferentiation makes for confusion between self and other, not knowing who the self is. Conscious development of psychological functions leads to the ability to be both different from and the same as others in a purposeful way.

Individuation

As I discuss in Chapter Two, Jung's concept of individuation has now become an important way of understanding transformative learning theory. Jung says that individuation is "a process of *differentiation* having for its goal the development of the individual personality" (Jung, [1921] 1971, p. 448). Individuation is a transformative process, one in which we bring the unconscious into consciousness and develop a dialogue with that aspect of our self, come to a better understanding of our shadow, become aware of our animus or anima (masculine or feminine soul), realize the influence of archetypes, and learn to see how we engage in projection. Sharp (2001) describes individuation as a circular odyssey or spiral, a journey where the aim is to get back to where you started, but knowing where you have been. We essentially remain who we are, but through the journey of individuation, we come to know who that self is.

In relation to psychological type theory, one aspect of individuation is the clarification of psychological preferences—developing a clear profile of preferences—which can then, in turn, be consciously developed. In transformative learning theory, psychological preferences are one type of habit of mind on which we may engage in critical questioning. At the same time, our preferences influence the way in which we engage in that questioning. And to go one step further, clarifying and developing preferences through the lifelong journey of individuation is transformative. In the remainder of this chapter, I discuss the second of these connections—how our psychological type preferences may influence the way we experience transformation.

Transformative Learning and Psychological Type

Perhaps one of the reasons researchers and theorists have sought to expand Mezirow's (2000) conceptualization of transformative learning theory is that Mezirow's approach is one of reason, a process comfortable to individuals with a preference for the thinking function, but seen as limiting to someone who is more intuitive or has an inclination toward the feeling function. I often speculate on the psychological type preferences of those who write about transformative learning. In this section of the chapter, I first go through the facets of transformation proposed by Mezirow, then turn to some of the elaborations on his theory.

Reaction to a Disorienting Event

Whether it is a life crisis or hearing a point of view different from one's own, people respond in different ways to potentially disorienting events. This has to do with the content of the event, the circumstances under which it is encountered, and the place where a person is in life, but I think it also has to do with psychological type preferences. People with a preference for the feeling function would seem to be those who would be most sensitive to encountering values different from their own. They are in tune with their environment and the reactions of others. Wanting to maintain that relationship, they are likely to be responsive to social norms, the opinions and questions of others, and issues raised in the media.

Individuals who have a preference for thinking, whether the thinking is introverted or extraverted, have strong principles and points of view that are not easily shaken. An alternative viewpoint is likely to be dismissed without a second thought unless it is accompanied by a logical and convincing argument. Even there, the person may be more likely to respond with a counterargument than to question his or her own assumptions. I also suspect that in the face of more traumatic disorienting events, a person who prefers the thinking function is likely to cling to strong principles in order to get through the situation.

People who prefer sensing or intuition would be sensitive to disorienting events, but in different ways. Intuitive people are likely to respond enthusiastically to the possibilities and opportunities for change—losing a job opens up the possibility of many other jobs. When the sensing function is dominant, the person relies on routines and things happening as they have happened before, so it seems reasonable to expect that he or she would be shaken by an unexpected turn of events.

Critical Reflection and Critical Self-Reflection

Critical reflection—critically questioning the values, assumptions, and perspectives presented in the world—is the purview of extraverted thinking. This is what it means to use the extraverted thinking function. Coming up with alternative points of view would be a natural process for someone with strong extraverted intuition, but the reflective part would be less pronounced unless that person had thinking as an auxiliary function. The ideal person for engaging in critical reflection would be someone with extraverted thinking as a dominant function and extraverted intuition as a secondary function. People who prefer feeling may adapt rather than question, and those who have a strong extraverted sensing function may focus on comparing the current experience with a past experience in order to solve the problem (this may look like reflection to an observer, but it is a different psychological process).

Undergoing self-examination and conducting a critical assessment of internalized assumptions should come more easily to people who tend toward introversion, especially introverted thinking. All introverted types have an inner focus and, in a sense, are interested in exploring their sense of self, but whether or not the process could be called "reflection" for those who are going by feeling, sensing, or intuition is debatable. Introspection, yes, reflection, perhaps not. But for those people whose thinking is inner-directed, this activity is a natural part of their being.

People who have a strong tendency toward the extraverted side would have difficulty with self-reflection unless they deliberately moved to the introverted part of their psychological profile. This can be encouraged through activities such as journal writing or meditation, but such activities do not come easily to a strongly extraverted person.

Discourse

Mezirow (1991) argues that participation in critical discourse is essential to transformative learning. "We all depend on consensual validation to establish the meaning of our assertions, especially in the communicative domain of learning, and . . . an ideal set of conditions for participation in critical discourse is implicit in the very nature of human communication" (p. 198). He reiterates this point of view when he examines the nature of reasoning within the context of discourse (Mezirow, 2003a). Although this point of view can be contested (perhaps we need to understand each other but not necessarily agree), if we stay with Mezirow's definition of discourse—one based on Habermas's notion that rationality is inherent in the use of language—then it would again be those learners who have a preference for thinking, especially extraverted thinking, who would find this a natural process.

Mezirow (2003a) does go on to say that having an open mind, listening empathetically, bracketing premature judgment, seeking common ground, and having the qualities of emotional intelligence are assets for participating in discourse. Some of these characteristics go with intuition (having an open mind, avoiding premature judgment) and others with the feeling function (listening empathetically, seeking common ground).

People who are strongly introverted may find discourse hard. When stimuli from the external world need to be processed internally as they do with introversion, this takes time. Introverted people often report that by the time they have formulated a response, the dialogue has moved on to another topic. Online discourse overcomes this obstacle (Lin and Cranton, 2004) but may introduce others.

Revision of Habits of Mind

Engaging in critical reflection and participating in rational discourse do not guarantee transformative learning. It is the revision of a habit of mind that makes the experience transformative. Sometimes people question, reflect, and discuss, but do not experience any fundamental changes as a result of this process. This may be a function of culture, society, family, or the workplace, but it may also be a function of psychological and learning preferences.

Individuals who have a preference for extraverted thinking may prefer not to revise habits of mind because they have a deep urge to stand by their principles and "truths." Those who are more introverted in their thinking may reluctantly revise perspectives based on new knowledge or an awareness of flaws in logic, but may not want to consider others' values or opinions in this process.

Following psychological type theory, it would seem that people who prefer the feeling function would readily revise their habits of mind—not through a process of critical reflection, but through a need to be in harmony with others' values. For a person with this preference, this is not a simple chameleon-like adaptation to others' views; it is a genuine shift in order to be at one with another. When feeling is more introverted, a subjective interpretation of the world is central, and perspective transformation would be an intense, inner process.

When a person has sensing as a dominant function of living, either extraverted or introverted, the revision of a habit of mind would be most likely to occur as a result of immersion into a different situation, one that provides completely fresh sensations such as a change in environment or culture. It is difficult to understand the intuitive mind in the context of this rational approach to transformation of habits of mind. I suspect that the extrarational approach to transformative learning better describes the experience of an individual with this preference.

Extrarational Transformative Learning

Jung's ([1921] 1971) view of psychological processes such as individuation is fundamentally extrarational in nature. We do not consciously choose one or the other, and we cannot develop inferior functions through critical reflection. At the core of individuation is establishing and maintaining a dialogue with the unconscious dimensions of the self, and this is not rational reflection as Mezirow describes it.

As I mention in Chapter Three, the psychological preferences of those who write about and do research on transformative learning theory may well influence the perspective within which they choose to work. Theorists as well as learners have different ways of seeing the world. The extrarational approach to transformation is based on an intuitive and imaginative understanding of learning and change. It transcends rationality and gives power and deep meaning to the connection between the self and the world. It nurtures the soul; it pays attention to the emotional and spiritual aspects of everyday occurrences.

It seems clear that individuals who have a preference for intuition, extraverted and introverted, would be more likely to experience transformative learning in an extrarational way. Perhaps having a combination of intuition and feeling as preferred functions would bring a learner closest to experiencing transformation in the way that Dirkx (1997, 2000) describes.

Relational Transformative Learning

In the relational or connected approach to transformative learning theory, people are seen as learning through relationships with others, integrative and holistic ways of seeing the world, understanding others' points of view (rather than debating them), empathic listening, and nurturing and caring. Individuals who have a preference for the feeling function, especially extraverted feeling, would be more likely to experience transformation in this way. This preference leads people to choose harmony over conflict and values-based judgments over logical, analytical judgments.

Belenky and Stanton's (2000) description of Connected Knowers is helpful in this respect. The more Connected Knowers disagree, the more they try to understand how the other feels, the more they make an effort to enter into another's frame of mind. This could be the crux of the transformative experience—entering into another's frame of mind with empathy rather than critically questioning or challenging points of view as is at the heart of Mezirow's (2003a, 2003b) perspective.

Summary

It is widely accepted in adult education theory and practice that learners have varying preferences and styles of learning. Jung's model of psychological types provides one powerful and comprehensive way of understanding individual differences. Jung describes people as having different attitudes toward the world: the extraverted attitude entails direct interaction with people, events, situations, and information, and the introverted attitude allows for indirect stimulation from the world but mainly consists of subjective inner-oriented processes. Psychological type theory also incorporates two preferences in making judgments: the use of logic (thinking) and the use of values (feeling). Finally, Jung describes two ways of perceiving: through the reality of the senses and through intuition. Everyone has attitudes and preferences of different strengths as well as dominant and auxiliary functions that work together in various ways.

The process of transformative learning varies among people of different psychological type profiles. The components of transformative learning theory that I examine include reaction to a disorienting event, critical reflection and critical self-reflection, discourse, and revision of habits of mind. The language of Mezirow's approach to transformative learning theory is most consistent with a preference for the psychological type function of thinking, but people with that preference may also be ones who are the most unwilling to let go of their deeply embedded principles and assumptions. I briefly discuss two of the alternative approaches to transformative learning theory, extrarational transformation and relational transformation. Based on the theoretical descriptions, it seems that individuals with a preference for intuition would be more likely to engage in the imaginative, holistic, extrarational experience and those with a preference for feeling would go through a relational or connected transformation.

6

Educator Roles

It is not surprising that adult educators doubt, question, and revise their roles continually. The literature bombards us with all the things we are supposed to be: experts, resource people, facilitators, counselors, mentors, models, reformers, and activists. We read that we should love our subject, share our enthusiasm and passion, be knowledgeable, consider learners' needs, organize and structure learning activities in a clear way, be good listeners, establish a supportive learning climate, motivate learners, use humor, challenge students' perspectives to encourage critical thinking, promote involvement, provide positive feedback, use learners as resources, and consider learning styles, to name just a few suggestions available in the literature.

As the adult education literature becomes more sophisticated and complex, so do the demands on the practitioner. Gone are the easy and safe days of the simple humanist approach of setting up a comfortable learning environment and meeting the needs of learners. Now we learn that we need to unmask power, challenge ideologies, and racialize criticality (Brookfield, 2005). And, as is our topic here, we need to foster transformative learning, but not only that, we need to be aware of a variety of interpretations of transformative learning theory and understand how they apply to different individuals. No wonder practitioners whose attention and passion is focused on working with their learners begin to feel alienated by the critiques and demands of some of the literature.

In this chapter, I rely on the framework used in Chapter One—technical, practical, and emancipatory knowledge—to discuss educator roles that promote the acquisition or construction of each kind of knowledge. As Mezirow (2000) suggests, transformative learning theory redefines Habermas's emancipatory domain as the transformative process that pertains in both instrumental and communicative learning. The teaching of technical skills can also be approached from a more emancipatory and transformative perspective. I then turn to the centrality of power issues in fostering transformative learning; since transformative learning is about gaining freedom from constraints, limited perspectives, and oppressive circumstances, it follows that helping people learn how to exercise power must be a part of our responsibilities as educators. Finally, I explore educator authenticity. If we believe in transformation as a primary goal of education, this view characterizes our relationship with students, with the content, with the context, and with ourselves. Thinking about authenticity then is a part of thinking about transformative education.

Educator Roles and Technical Knowledge

There can be no doubt that our way of teaching depends in part on what we are teaching. The current adult education literature places little emphasis on the acquisition of technical knowledge, but this is what many people do—help others learn technical knowledge and skills. In my regular summer school teaching, where a good proportion of the participants are trades and technology instructors, people express great relief that I acknowledge their teaching as at least existing (something they do not necessarily encounter in other education courses). I am also very conscious of how instrumental learning (the acquisition of technical knowledge) spirals into transformative learning and how, in turn, transformative learning can lead people to the further need for instrumental learning. Learning how to be a carpenter has as much potential to lead people into a deep shift in the way they see themselves and the world around them as does studying critical theory or exploring childhood traumas through narrative.

Working with technical knowledge leads to certain educator roles. While technical knowledge could be discovered or constructed, it would be a time-consuming and foolish endeavor. Individuals who deny that any knowledge exists "out there" and promote relativism and constructivism as approaches to technical learning have probably not taught many plumbing courses. I do not mean that critical thinking is not a part of working with technical knowledge; indeed it is. Students learn to critically examine and question techniques and diagnostic procedures, and not accept information at face value, but there is a body of knowledge that is learned, practiced, and applied.

In this context, educators are *experts and authorities* in their subject area. They are experienced and practiced trades people and technicians. The educator describes himself or herself as a mechanic, a botanist, or a physiotherapist. The expert selects the content, orders the content into an agenda or outline, selects materials and resources, and presents the content in a primarily instructor-centered fashion. It is the educator who decides when the students have mastered the content.

Educators who work with technical knowledge also often see themselves as a *designer* of instruction. The educator considers the prior learning and experience of the learners, writes objectives for the instruction, arranges the topics in a sequence to make learning progress from one level to another, designs strategies that are appropriate for the learning, and constructs evaluative techniques.

Typically, instruction in technical knowledge follows a sequence in which information is presented, demonstrations of the application of the knowledge are given, and learners have the opportunity for extended practice. In some subject areas, problem solving or problem-based learning are commonly used methods. Learning is often hands-on or experiential in nature. Critical thinking in terms of questioning procedures, troubleshooting, and finding alternative ways of accomplishing the same task are often encouraged.

We do not usually think of technical knowledge as the basis for transformative learning, but it seems that it has as much potential to lead to a transformative experience as does learning in any domain. My mother, who grew up in the city of Amsterdam in the 1930s, had no opportunity or need to learn to drive a car, but when she was later living in a remote, rural area of Alberta where the nearest neighbor was two miles away and her husband was out in the grain fields all day, her life was constrained and controlled by her inability to go anywhere. She never did have the courage to try to learn to drive, but I often think of the transformative potential that set of technical skills would have had for her. When I acquired the technical ability to make good photographs, the way I saw the world was changed. When people learn the fundamental, technical competencies of reading and writing, they often experience their more ready access to information as powerful and liberating. In a historical piece, Selman (1989) describes how adult literacy educators in the 1800s were seen as radicals in that they were working against the status quo to help people gain greater access to information.

Though the acquisition of technical knowledge is not necessarily transformative in itself, I see it has having the potential to provide a foundation for transformation. We artificially separate kinds of knowledge into categories so as to better understand patterns of learning, and this is useful to do, but we also need to pull those strands back together and understand how each contributes to and is intertwined with the other.

Educator Roles and Communicative Knowledge

When the learning goals are for students to construct knowledge about themselves, others, and social norms, the primary educator role is one of *facilitator* of a learner-directed or a codirected (teacher and learner) process. The facilitator responds to the needs of the learners, fosters a meaningful group process, provides support and encouragement, builds a trusting relationship with learners, helps challenge people's assumptions and beliefs, and accepts and respects learners. Brookfield and Preskill (1999) emphasize how the facilitator of discussion can, among other things,

- Help students explore a diversity of perspectives

- Increase students' awareness of and tolerance for ambiguity

- Help students recognize and investigate assumptions

- Encourage attentive, respectful listening

- Develop appreciation for differences

- Show respect for students' voices and experiences

- Affirm students as co-creators of knowledge

- Develop habits of collaborative learning

- Lead to transformation (pp. 22–23)

Vella (2002) makes similar points in her twelve principles of dialogue education. She underlines the importance of relationships between teacher and learner and among learners, respect for learners as decision makers, teamwork and group work, and learner engagement.

In communicative learning, the educator often acts as a *resource person* and *manager*. The educator assists the learning process by referring people to materials, readings, experiences, or other individuals. He or she might also arrange visits to a field site and organize special events.

Since communicative knowledge is usually coconstructed with educator and learners, teachers may become a *mentor* or a *model*.

The model role is more common when the educator-learner inter-action occurs in the workplace where the learner identifies with attributes and job functions of the educator. The mentor role may be more likely in longer-term interactions. Mentoring is fostered by a relationship that encourages trust, openness, personal disclosure, and closeness. The model or mentor displays a love for the subject area, expresses contagious enthusiasm, encourages personal inter-actions, and is open and authentic.

Since communicative knowledge is concerned with how we see ourselves and the social world that shapes us, the potential for it to become transformative (or emancipatory) is great. Our sociolinguis-tic habits of mind (see Chapter Two) are often called into question when we are exposed to new perspectives in the communicative domain. At the time of my writing this, the tsunami disaster in southeast Asia has led millions of people in the Western world to come to a new awareness of cultures and context with which they were unfamiliar previously. On an individual level, something as seemingly simple as returning to school after a prolonged absence can lead people to see themselves and others in a way that may be discrepant with their values and beliefs, which can, in turn, lead to transformation. The facilitator of communicative knowledge needs to be aware of this possibility.

Educator Roles and Emancipatory Learning

When the educator's goal is to set up an environment and learning context in which people critically question their habits of mind in order to become open to alternatives, it is emancipatory learning that he or she is fostering. Although the debate that began in 1991 when Mezirow wrote, "adult learning transforms meaning perspec-tives not society" (p. 208) continues today, there seems to be a stronger sense that transformative learning theory can be more holistic in nature and incorporate both individual perspective trans-formation and social transformation without arguing about which must come first. The primary educator role for fostering emancipatory learning is that of *reformist*. (I use this word in a way that is similar in meaning to the radical philosophy of adult education as described by Merriam and Brockett [1997]). The reformer sees education as a means of helping individuals and groups exercise their own power, which may result in personal and social change. Depending on one's philosophy of education, there are other, related roles that can be a part of encouraging emancipatory learning.

The educator following Freire's writings (1970) is often a *co-learner*. He or she works with learners and tries to find out about their lives and experiences even as learners may be questioning their values. When this happens, students become co-teachers, and knowledge is created collaboratively. For example, the educator working to increase literacy does not simply teach reading as a technical skill, nor does he assume that people will come to him when they are ready to learn to read; rather, he shares the experiences of the learners, learns about their culture and values, and works within that perspective toward his goal. Similarly, the group leader working in a women's shelter learns about the women's experiences as she works with them to question their views of those experiences. The educator who is a co-learner is a participant in the process of learning—discovering, challenging, and changing. There is an atmosphere of mutual trust and respect, authenticity, and a sense of enthusiasm and interest in others as well as challenges of others' points of view.

The educator fostering emancipatory learning may also be a *provocateur*, one who challenges, stimulates, and provokes critical thinking. Brookfield is especially well-known for his helpful writing on how to teach critical thinking. In his earlier book, *Developing Critical Thinkers*, Brookfield (1991) provides educators with a variety of strategies for stimulating critical thinking. More recently he emphasizes that this kind of teaching is inherently political in that it is intended to help people learn how to replace capitalism with democratic socialism. Teaching critical thinking is not and cannot be neutral—the point is to change the world (Brookfield, 2005). Teaching critically is as much about what we teach as it is a method.

The provocateur helps ensure that the norms governing rational discourse are maintained as a goal and encourages the group support that is needed when learners experience challenges to their beliefs and values. The provocateur will guide students into an awareness of limiting habits of mind and help them deal with the discrepancies between their expressed values and their actions. Strategies for doing this are the topics of Chapters Seven, Eight, and Nine.

Power

In the first edition of this book, I drew on literature from the late 1980s (for example, Yukl, 1989) to understand how power is a part of adult educator roles. From this perspective, position power is associated with the formal position a person is in, and it consists of formal authority, control over resources and rewards, control over punishment, control over information, and ecological or environmental control. Personal power has as its source expertise, friendship and loyalty, and charisma. It is partly based on the personal characteristics of the individual and partly on the relationship the individual develops with others. Political power stems from control over decision processes, coalitions, cooptation, and institutionalization.

The literature in adult education has long emphasized learner empowerment and the necessity of the educator's giving up power, especially position power, in order to accomplish this goal. This was my position in the previous edition of this book.

Perceptions of power have shifted in recent years as Foucault's (1980) and others' ideas about power have been introduced into adult education, and perhaps especially since writers such as Brookfield (2001, 2005) have helped ordinary readers understand Foucault's work. In this section, I rely on Brookfield's translations of Foucault's analysis of power.

Foucault argues that sovereign power—that which is exercised from above by an authority, or position power as I called it earlier—has been replaced by disciplinary power in contemporary society. Disciplinary power is exercised by people "on themselves and others in their lives" (Brookfield, 2001, p. 1) and is based on knowing the inside of people's minds. The emphasis we place on individual achievement, autonomy, self-direction, learning arranged in discrete stages, and the fragmentation of curriculum is a demonstration of disciplinary power whereby people are sorted, classified, and differentiated. Power is omnipresent and is exercised continually in all details of everyday life. Disciplinary power exists in the way eye contact is made between teacher and student, how the message is conveyed as to who should speak, seating arrangements (including the common circle), and the form of speech that is considered acceptable. According to this view, power is exercised rather than possessed and is all-pervasive rather than held by an elite group and used to repress others. As such, it is impossible to "give it away."

In our society, individuals discipline themselves. This is an aspect of disciplinary power that Foucault calls self-surveillance. We watch ourselves because we want to stay close to the norm, to fit in, to be accepted and approved. Based on his work in prisons, Foucault also describes compulsory visibility in which a person can be watched by others but is never certain he or she is being watched at any one time. This is not only the case in prisons. In modern society and institutions, technology has led to a state in which everyone is visible in some sense with cameras recording their entrance into stores and banks, computers monitoring and recording their every transaction, marketing firms tracking purchases and preferences, and government departments keeping files on individual lives. We are never sure just when we are being watched, so it is better to behave as though we are being watched at this moment.

Brookfield (2005) draws on his own experience as a learner to illustrate how participating in what looks on the surface to be a democratic, empowering discussion can be a competitive intellectual exercise in which students suspect they are supposed to speak frequently and brilliantly but do not quite know how to do so. This is not to say that discussion is always perceived this way by participants or that truly collaborative construction of knowledge cannot occur. Our classrooms can be based on relationships of trust and respect, not fear, and power can be used to increase power, not oppress. My goal here is not to substitute one view of power relations for another, but rather to encourage educators to "unmask" or question their understanding of power and examine their practice carefully for ways in which power is hidden behind surface forms that appear to be free.

In spite of the seeming negativity of Foucault's analysis, his view is that power is pleasurable and productive (Brookfield, 2001). The exercise of power produces responses, forms knowledge, and informs discourse. One of the desirable effects it has is resistance, as it is through exploring resistance to power that we can understand what power relations are about. There is no power without resistance to it. Where there is dominance, there is resistance to that dominance. So, unlike a situation where sovereign power (complete dominance with no possibility of resistance) reigns, our society's disciplinary power allows individual acts of opposition.

What does all of this tell us about power in the various educator roles I describe here? Brookfield (2001) reminds us that we can no longer divide educators into the "good guys (democratic adult educators who subvert dominant power through experiential, dialogic practices) and bad guys (behaviourally inclined trainers who reproduce dominant ideology and practices by forcing corporate agendas on adult learners)" (p. 22). We are used to thinking of the expert, authoritarian, or designer role as one in which the educator exercises power through making decisions about content, learning activities, and evaluation strategies. But the facilitator, whom we assume to be democratic and participatory, uses strategies that embody disciplinary power.

The inevitable discussion circle puts students under the surveillance of their peers; they are exposed and vulnerable, and their degree of participation is immediately noticeable. Learning journals and learning contracts allow educators "inside the heads" of learners and encourage self-surveillance as people try to write what they expect the teacher to want or, in other words, to stay close to the norm. They may even feel called upon to invent dramatic insights and experiences or to present ordinary experiences in an exaggerated way. In discussions, students feel obligated to live up to the (often implicit) idea of what constitutes "good discussion."

I recall an incident from my practice about one year ago. We were a small group, perhaps twelve students and two facilitators. As sometimes happens, there were two or three participants who were quiet. We sat in the typical circle for our discussions. The discussions were lively and interesting; it did not concern me that a couple of people chose to listen rather than speak. But it did bother some members of the group. Each time we asked for formative feedback at the end of the day, one or two people mentioned the quiet ones. This feedback was distributed back to the group (surveillance power at its finest), but the speaking patterns did not change. The feedback grew more pointed—"you are depriving the group of your ideas and experiences," read one comment. Finally a participant approached me privately and asked me to "do something" about "those people who won't talk." I explained that I preferred not to require anyone to speak, and he expressed strong sentiments to the contrary. They do not have the right to stay quiet, he argued; they owe the group their ideas. We did not resolve the issue between us, though it colored the process for everyone, I think. The whole group was aware of the pressure from "someone" for others to speak. I am still not sure how this could have been managed so as to encourage or at least allow everyone to feel safe to contribute in the ways they wanted to, without pressure to speak or exercise voice.

In the reformist or provocateur role of fostering emancipatory learning, surveillance power may be embodied in a different way. Brookfield (2001) suggests that "liberatory practices can actually work subtly to perpetuate existing power relations" and participatory approaches can "inadvertently reinforce the discriminatory practices they seek to challenge" (p. 222). One example that immediately comes to mind is the attempt to recognize women's learning and women's voices by labeling or stereotyping all women as relational learners. The intent is good, but the outcome is further marginalization. Even in a technique as simple as the critical incident, which is designed to help people articulate their underlying assumptions, people are called upon to make their "worst experiences" public—an example of the exercise of surveillance power (let me get inside your mind, and then I will "help" you). Becoming conscious of the power relations inherent in our daily practice as adult educators is essential.

Authenticity

In the midst of all this talk about taking on specific roles, where does the teacher as a person come in? Can we just automatically become whatever we need to become in order to facilitate learning? I first became interested in authenticity in teaching through exploring psychological type theory (see Chapter Five) as a way of understanding students' learning preferences. If students vary in the way they prefer to learn, teachers surely vary just as much in the way they prefer to teach. I had long advocated that there is no best way of teaching—that we need to consider the nature of the knowledge we are working with, the context of teaching, and the characteristics of our students. But I went on to think about teachers' psychological type preferences and began work on a book I initially called *No Bad Teachers*, a title that the publisher wisely discouraged. This eventually became *Becoming an Authentic Teacher in Higher Education* (2001).

Dissatisfied with armchair speculation about authenticity, a colleague and I conducted a three-year study of how educators describe authenticity and how they become authentic in their practice (Cranton and Carusetta, 2004a, 2004b). Interviews, observations of teaching, and focus group discussions with twenty-two educators led us to describe five facets of authenticity: self-awareness, awareness of others, relationships, context, and critical reflection.

Educators spoke about their awareness of themselves as people and as teachers, how they came to be a teacher, what that meant for them, their values, their passions, the conflicts they experienced between the realities of teaching and their values, and the ways in which they brought themselves as people into their practice. Teaching was a passion for many. They spoke of it as a calling or a vocation, as something that gave meaning to their life.

Participants in the project recognized the importance of understanding others as a part of their own authenticity. They showed a strong interest in and awareness of their students' characteristics, needs, and learning styles. Some educators also were aware of and concerned with students' personal problems and lives outside of the classroom, but others preferred to stay more distant.

The most commonly discussed facet of authenticity had to do with the relationship between teacher and student. This was broadly defined to include helping students learn, caring for students, engaging in dialogue, and being aware of exercising power. Included in this is the ability to enjoy the expression of others' power. Educators talked about the nature of their relationships with students, and many project participants struggled with where the boundary of their relationships should be, especially in light of their responsibilities for evaluation and grading. There was discussion of how open educators should be about their own lives in their interactions with students. Underlying many of our conversations was an intense and powerful sense of caring about students and their learning. We also found a variety of perceptions of how power contributed to or inhibited relationships between educators and students.

Being involved in relationships with others (colleagues, family, and friends) with whom they talked about teaching was also important to many participants. Being able to talk with others allowed them to maintain an integration of teaching, their personal life, and the rest of their professional life—something they associated with being authentic.

The context within which educators work influences their perceptions of themselves, their students, and their relationships with students. Context consists of several levels: the content of the teaching; the discipline or subject area; the physical classroom, including the size of the class and the room arrangement; the psychological environment within the learning group; the department in which people work and its norms and expectations; institutional norms and policies; and finally, the general community or culture and the roles people expect educators to maintain.

Critical reflection was a strong theme throughout our conversations with the educators who participated in our project. Many used the word "reflection," and there was a sense that people were critical of or questioning themselves, others, and social norms. However, at times, they were also relaying feelings, hunches, intuition, or insights from practice. Critical self-reflection and critical reflection on relationships with their students were the most common, but participants also reflected on student characteristics and the context of their teaching.

If we assume educator roles that are not congruent with our values, beliefs, and personality preferences, we are asking students to communicate with the role, not the person. Teaching is a specialized form of communication that has learning as its goal, and here, our special interest is in transformative learning. The better the relationship among the people, the more meaningful the communication will be. In thinking about how authentic teaching relies on relating with students, I often think of a quote from Hollis (2001). He writes, "the quality of all our relationships is a direct function of our relationship to ourselves," and "the best thing we can do for our relationships with others . . . is to render our relationship to ourselves more conscious" (p. 13). Jarvis (1992) says it more directly: "Authentic action is to be found when individuals freely act in such a way that they try to foster the growth and development of each other's being" (p. 113). Similarly, Belenky, Bond, and Weinstock's (1997) work in developmental leadership illustrates this kind of inclusive, caring connection among people who are working hard to understand each other as they are rather than as they could or should be.

In fostering transformative learning, we help create conditions whereby students will become conscious of their assumptions, beliefs, and perspectives; realize that there are alternative points of view; and begin to see their perspectives in a different way. Many kinds of events can precipitate such a process, as I discuss in Chapters Seven through Nine, but I suspect the authenticity of the educator contributes in an important way. Palmer (1998) has encouraged us to pay attention to developing our identity and integrity in all aspects of our practice. Becoming authentic is often transformative (Cranton and Carusetta, 2004b), as a person separates himself or herself from the collective norms. Not only does authenticity in teaching help create honest and open relationships with students, but it also serves as a model for learners working to define who they are.

Summary

Using the framework of technical, practical, and emancipatory knowledge, I discuss educator roles that promote the acquisition of each kind of knowledge from a transformative perspective. Educators who are helping students obtain technical or instrumental knowledge are most often experts and authorities in their subject area—people with years of practical experience and considerable theoretical expertise. They design the instruction by selecting the topics, arranging the best sequence of events, and choosing teaching and evaluation strategies that will best serve the learner. Although it might be possible for learners to discover or create knowledge themselves in this domain, it would not be practical or efficient in most cases. Technical knowledge often provides the basis for transformative learning in that it gives a learner the skills and knowledge that free them from constraints, change their concept of themselves as people, and perhaps redefine their notion of work.

Communicative knowledge is constructed with the help of an educator as facilitator. Interactive methods, collaborative learning, dialogue, and group activities help students work through an understanding of themselves, others, and the social world they live in. When people create new personal and social knowledge, they often go on to question their pre-existing perspectives and move toward transformative learning.

Emancipatory knowledge is fostered through a variety of reformist educator roles. Critical questioning, the presentation of diverse points of view, the examination of existing social norms, and the exploration of alternative and radical perspectives helps students become more open in their views and free from the constraints of unquestioned assumptions.

Power relations are embodied in all of our teaching and learning interactions. In this chapter, I rely on Brookfield's understanding of Foucault's work on disciplinary power and the subset of self-surveillance. Rather than giving away power, as we have long talked about in adult education, we need to learn to work with the power we and our learners exercise in all of the ordinary interactions of the classroom.

Finally, I turn and question the idea of educator roles by discussing the important role of authenticity in fostering transformative learning. Being an authentic educator involves having a good understanding of oneself and bringing that understanding into teaching, understanding and relating in a meaningful way with learners, being aware of the context of teaching, and engaging in critical reflection on practice. Not only does authenticity bring us to better connections with students, but it also models the transformative process itself.

7

Empowering Learners

Fostering "liberating conditions for making more autonomous and informed choices and developing a sense of self-empowerment is the cardinal goal of adult education" (Mezirow, 2000a, p. 26). "Adult educators create protected learning environments in which the conditions of social democracy necessary for transformative learning are fostered. This involves blocking out power relationships engendered in the structure of communication, including those traditionally existing between teachers and learners" (p. 31). Through emancipatory knowledge, the learner is freed from the constraints of unquestioned or inflexible ways of knowing; the learner is empowered or perhaps enfranchised. However, transformative learning cannot take place simply because either the educator or the learner decides that this is a goal of the learning experience. Engaging in the critical self-reflection that may lead to changes in a perspective is, in itself, a process that requires self-awareness, planning, skill, support, and discourse with others. Embedded in that list of requirements is a prerequisite that the learner already be empowered to some extent or at least be working in a context that is empowering and supportive.

As I discussed in Chapter Two, one of the ideal conditions of rational discourse is that the participants be free from coercion; another is that individuals have an equal opportunity to participate. If rational discourse is a key component of working toward transformative learning, as Mezirow suggests, then we can see that learner empowerment must accompany the entire process rather than be viewed as an outcome of a transformative experience. Even if discourse is not a necessary component of the process, it seems that the critical questioning of basic assumptions, values, and beliefs cannot easily take place when a person feels disempowered.

An illustration may be useful. Carmen has enrolled in her first course at the local adult education center. Her assumptions about authority are well developed and reinforced often. When she was in high school, she looked to her teacher for the right answers. As a parent, her children have relied on her for protection, guidance, and direction. In her community, she respects people in positions of authority and is admired for doing so. In her world, social roles are clear.

On the first day of Carmen's new course, she meets an instructor who provides a detailed and frighteningly difficult looking course outline. He reviews the criteria for evaluation in the course, emphasizing the importance of preparing for the certification examination. He advises students to obtain a copy of the fifth edition of the American Psychological Association (APA) manual, so they can start right away to use the proper writing and referencing styles. He says that he assumes everyone has a personal computer and a high-speed Internet connection. Carmen thinks momentarily of her restricted budget and wonders how much a high-speed connection might cost, but then she returns her attention to the teacher, who is now explaining that learning to be a critical thinker is a key component in adult education. "You are expected not only to read but to be critical of what you read," he remarks. "Everyone needs to be able to sift through all of the information available these days, and not just accept things because they are in print or on the news." He goes on, "And you will be expected not only to be critical of others' work but of your own work and your own thinking." The teacher discusses how they will work together as a group and emphasizes that everyone should feel completely free to interrupt him, ask questions, and express their views. He then gives his introductory lecture and, unfortunately, runs out of time, so the questions will have to wait until the next class.

This teacher—a composite of several teachers I have known—would say that he encourages learner empowerment. He uses interactive methods; he advocates critical thinking and critical self-reflection; his classroom is democratic. Yet from Carmen's perspective, who already sees her teacher as an authority based on her own social norms, there is only confusion and anxiety. Just yesterday, I received the following comment in response to a formative feedback check in my class: "All of this self-directed stuff is fine, but imposed deadlines would be helpful." What we think of as empowering is not necessarily what learners think is empowering.

Unfortunately, as Brookfield (2000) says, the word *empowerment* has been used so often in so many contexts that it has lost its distinctive meaning; it is "far removed from the words and actions of Paulo Freire or Myles Horton" (p. 141). I take this caution to heart, and attempt to use the term in accordance with its true meaning. In this chapter, I suggest we promote learner empowerment in at least four ways: by becoming conscious of power relations in our practice, by exercising power in responsible and meaningful ways, by helping learners exercise power through and in discourse, and by encouraging learner decision making. Finally, I consider how individual differences among learners need to be considered in our understanding of power and empowerment.

Awareness of Power Relations

Brookfield (2001) suggests that we use the point of resistance to understand power, as there are no power relations without resistances. An incident from a couple of years ago comes to mind when I think about what this means. I was facilitating a course on transformative learning in summer school. Students had the opportunity to design and lead various activities in the group if they wished to do so. I no longer remember the goal or the purpose of the activity led by this particular small group, but the activity itself stays clearly in my mind. Everyone had a name of a "famous character" taped on his or her back. Others could see the name, but the person who wore the sign did not know what it said. By asking questions of others, we were supposed to guess the name we wore. I asked many questions of many other participants, but I came no closer to guessing the name on my back. Finally, when I was the only one left (or perhaps that is only my memory, perhaps there were a few left who could not guess), they told me the name was "Big Bird." To the great amusement of everyone in the room, I asked what "Big Bird" was. I grew up without television and have consciously avoided television and the television culture throughout my life. Of course, I knew it was only a game and the students were well-intentioned and their laughter was affectionate, but I felt a sharp resistance to the activity and especially to the assumption made about all people having a knowledge of television. When one of the students leading the activity said, "We never dreamt that anyone wouldn't know who Big Bird was," I used the moment to talk about assumptions, but I can now understand this point of resistance as an entry into understanding power relations. I didn't like it one bit that I, the professor, felt foolish for not knowing a character that all children in North America know.

The student who commented that he or she would find imposed deadlines helpful in my class was showing resistance. Students who complain that not everyone has a chance to speak show resistance. Students who object that they have a right to be quiet show resistance. The typical facilitator response to such feedback is to try to make a change to overcome the problem, and this is fine, but when learner empowerment is our goal, can we use these opportunities to increase our awareness of power relations? What is the student who wants imposed deadlines really asking? Perhaps it is an attempt to find out what the hidden social norms really are? If the student is engaging in self-surveillance and wants to be sure to fit in with the norms of the class, how can this be done if the deadline isn't given? Surely, it is not acceptable to do the learning plan six months from now? How about six weeks? Six days? How am I using power when I refuse to say what is a reasonable time for completing this work? This kind of analysis can help the educator and the learners understand the power relations in the group.

In this same class, we talked about the discussion circle and questioned the assumption that it automatically promoted democratic interactions. In the days following that dialogue, students often pointed out ways in which the circle made them feel empowered or disempowered. Awareness of the issue led the way.

Brookfield (2001) suggests that "discussion as a way of learning that is quintessentially adult can be experienced by learners as performance theatre, a situation in which their acting is carefully watched" (p. 21). The unexpressed norms for good discussion are assumed to be known by the discussion leader, and participants monitor their own behavior and scan the environment for clues as to how they are being received. The facilitator participates in this by nodding, smiling, and somehow indicating what good discussion performance is. If the development of discussion norms was done by the group in an open way, perhaps self-surveillance and second guessing could be reduced. Making norms explicit and the responsibility of the group applies not only to discussion. If we pay attention to resistances, we may be able to see the power issue on the flip side of the coin each time.

Adult educators who have learner empowerment as a goal should be conscious of the power relations implicit in the strategies we have assumed to be power free. Learning journals, learning contracts, self-evaluation, and collaborative work do embody disciplinary power. This is not to say we should consider abandoning such methods, but rather that we need to become conscious of how power is exercised within our practice.

In exploring power, we also need to consider its irrational dimensions. As Sharp (2001) says, "People generally confuse self-knowledge with knowledge of their ego-personalities." Our power relationships often stem from our inner interests—unconscious fears, morally inferior wishes and motives, and childish fantasies and resentments. I sometimes become aware, for example, of a childish and rather desperate need to be liked as I am facilitating a group—a desire emerging from my shadow side. Issues of classroom control and management may have less to do with consciously creating an environment for learning than our unconscious need to be in control and in charge. Helping learners feel empowered requires educators to understand their own relationship with power, and this process is not always conscious or accessible through critical self-reflection.

Exercising Power Responsibly

Some manifestations of sovereign power (exercised from above by a clear authority figure) are obvious and are usually avoided or rejected by adult educators; for example, talking down to students, allowing no interruptions or questions, and maintaining complete control over resources, information, and rewards. Nevertheless, this isn't quite as straightforward as it appears. Teachers are perceived to have a role of authority in most social groups; it is the authority that comes automatically from holding the position of teacher that is the most troublesome here. I am no longer advocating that educators are able to or should give up power, for this is not possible, but I do think that we need to do our best to ensure that others do not perceive us as exercising sovereign power when it is not our intent to do so. To this end, I draw on the material in the first edition of this book (Cranton, 1994, pp. 148–153) to make several suggestions for exercising power responsibly:

- Reduce the trappings of formal authority such as standing in front of the group and using a title.

- Avoid being in the position of providing all of the answers, having the right answers, making all decisions, and controlling everything that learners do.

- Ensure that access to resources is easily available by helping people use the Internet, library, and electronic library; do not be the only source of material and information.

- Lessen the disempowering effect of grading by using some combination of strategies such as learning con-tracts, self-evaluation, peer evaluation, and flexible learning projects.

- Involve students in controlling the learning environ-ment—both the physical arrangement of the room and the group norms and activities.

- Remain open and explicit about all strategies; learners should know what the educator is doing and why.

- Acknowledge and use expertise as a source of power that builds credibility and trust and serves as a founda-tion for helping learners question assumptions.

- Develop open and authentic connections with students in which respect and loyalty are meaningful compo-nents of the power relations.

Foucault maintains that disciplinary power—that which is exer-cised by people on themselves and others—has replaced sovereign power in our society and is exercised continually in all interactions. Disciplinary power is based on knowing the insides of people's minds; it is not deliberately engineered. A normalizing gaze keeps people in line, behaving as they are supposed to behave according to the social norms of the community or, in this case, classroom. Learners watch themselves (self-surveillance) in order to be an acceptable part of the educational community. How can educators exercise disciplinary power responsibly?

Brookfield (2001, 2005) suggests that we expose the mechanisms of control, revealing and undermining power that is invisible and insidious. We cannot choose whether or not to exercise power, but we can seek out the manifestations of power and address them directly. We can talk to our learners about how power is exercised in discussions and learning activities. We can observe the ways in which we reward and shape the kind of participation we expect to see and then be open about that process. We can seek learners' help in recognizing and interpreting disciplinary power and self-surveillance. We can assist learners to recognize that they, too, are agents of power and have the capacity for subverting dominant power relations.

Empowerment Through Discourse

Although all theorists do not agree (see Chapter Three), Mezirow (2003a) sees discourse as central to transformative learning. Discourse refers to "dialogue involving the assessment of beliefs, feelings, and values" (p. 59). Participants in discourse try on the perspectives of others and adapt communication to another person's perspective. Having an open mind, listening carefully and empathically, seeking common ground, and suspending judgment help learners assess alternative beliefs as they participate in discourse. Equal participation and freedom from coercion are central to discourse serving as a vehicle for empowerment.

There is something disturbingly circular about this. Mezirow (2003a, 2004) clearly states that the "hungry, desperate, sick, destitute, and intimidated . . . cannot participate fully and freely in discourse" (2003a, p. 60). And, "the only alternatives to critical-dialectical discourse for assessing and choosing among beliefs are the appeal to tradition, an authority figure, or the use of force" (p. 60). If discourse is central to empowerment, but the disempowered cannot participate fully and freely in discourse, I wonder how empowerment occurs. Mezirow goes on to say that two capabilities are indispensable to learning to participate in discourse—the capability of critical self-reflection as described by Kegan (2000) and the capability of reflective judgment (the assessment of assumptions and expectations supporting beliefs, values, and feelings). The highest stage of reflective judgment (King and Kitchener, 1994) is one in which individuals engage in abstract thinking about and critiquing of their own as well as others' perspectives. Research associates these capabilities with age and education, with only college graduates reaching the highest stage of reflective judgment (considered indispensable to participation in discourse).

My concern is that this way of understanding transformative learning seems to be exclusive. Mezirow (2003a) does say that "overcoming the threat of exclusion constitutes a significant epistemological rationale for adult educators to commit themselves to economic, cultural, and social action initiatives" (p. 60), but meanwhile, I worry about the individuals with whom so many of us work in labor education, literacy education, social services, and so forth. If we follow this particular line of Mezirow's thinking, the practice of educators such as Moses Coady, Myles Horton, and Paulo Freire would not have led to transformative experiences. The alternative theoretical perspectives I describe in Chapter Three allow us to step around the problem by minimizing the role of rational discourse, but I would like to maintain that we can keep discourse (or perhaps dialogue) and still engage all who are ready and willing to be engaged.

Some possible strategies for encouraging equal participation in discourse follow; their appropriateness depends on the context of the interaction.

- Find provocative ways to stimulate dialogue from different perspectives—controversial statements, readings from contradictory points of view, or structured group activities that lead people to see alternatives.

- Develop discourse procedures within the group. In order to meet its goal of validity testing, discourse needs to stay focused. Group members can be encouraged to take on the roles of checking and controlling

the direction of the discourse, ensuring equal participation, and watching out for coercion and persuasion.

- Avoid making dismissive statements or definitive
  summaries. To minimize the role of disciplinary power
  and self-surveillance, the educator must be careful not
  to shape the discussion through implicit regulatory
  functions.

- Be conscious of nonverbal communication such as
  smiles, nods, and eye contact that can give clues as to
  what the educator is approving.

- Encourage quiet time for reflection within any exchange.

Learner Decision Making

The notion that students should have control over decisions to do
with their learning has been with us for some time, but it remains a
complex issue. Learner empowerment in an environment where the
learner is told what to learn, how, and by when seems unlikely. The
early adult educators, who often had a social action agenda, helped
people set up learning environments and provided resources and
guidance, but they did not determine the content and purpose of the
educational process. In the 1960s, educational researchers examined
what they then called "learner control," comparing it to traditional
teacher-controlled conditions (for example, see Campbell, 1964);
in retrospect this was a misguided application of experimental research in that no characteristics of either teachers or learners were
considered, but it is interesting that such research took place at all.
In the 1970s, in a time when instructional design models formed
the backbone of curriculum planning, learner control was applied
to each of the components of the design process—diagnosing needs,
setting objectives, sequencing and pacing, choosing methods and

materials, and evaluating progress (for example, see Della-Dora and Blanchard, 1979).

Knowles's (1975) approach to self-directed learning followed the instructional design model of that time, and although he added the use of learning contracts, the process was essentially one of the student becoming a designer of his or her own instructional activities.

In the 1980s and early 1990s, self-directed learning was explored in a variety of ways—as a personal characteristic of learners, as a method of teaching, and, with Candy's (1991) book, a multidimensional construct. Based on an exhaustive review of the literature to that date, Candy identified four facets of self-directed learning: autonomy (a personal characteristic), self-management (making decisions about one's educational path), learner control (making decisions about learning within a formal setting), and autodidaxy (self-initiated learning projects outside a formal setting). Jarvis (1992) pointed out the paradox "that while the ideology of society is that people are free and autonomous, a great deal of human learning is other-directed and certainly other-controlled" (pp. 141–142).

In recent years, critical theory has informed our practice. Brookfield (2005) outlines the tasks of critical theory:

- *Challenging ideology*, where ideologies are embedded in our language, social norms, and cultural expectations. They are reified—they appear as givens and, as such, are difficult to dig out and examine.

- *Confronting hegemony*, with hegemony describing those things we have accepted as natural and commonsensical, but actually work against our best interests and in the interests of those who wish to retain control or protect the status quo.

- *Unmasking power*, specifically using Foucault's concepts of disciplinary power and self-surveillance.

- *Overcoming alienation*, where alienation is a product of living in a way that is incongruent with who we are, when we commodify ourselves and act as automatons.

- *Learning liberation*, where, calling on Marcuse's concept of one-dimensional thought, Brookfield explains how autonomous thinking leads to critiquing the systems that manipulate us.

- *Reclaiming reason*, the process by which we understand how preconscious, taken-for-granted perceptions determine how we experience reality.

- And finally, *practicing democracy*.

Each of these tasks is relevant to students' involvement in decision making about their learning, but it is the idea of one-dimensional learning that seems to explain best for me the seeming paradox of learners wanting freedom and wanting to be told what to do. According to Brookfield (2005), Marcuse believes that we "learn our own servitude and that we have learned to love our condition of oppression . . . [as a result of being] lulled into stupefaction by the possession of consumer goods" (p. 188). We have been manipulated to feel happy, and if we knew it, we would want to liberate ourselves. It is one-dimensional thought that is the mechanism of control. One-dimensional thought is focused on how to make the current system better, rather than to critique that system. Divergent thinking is discouraged; we are indoctrinated to not question and to stay in the existing framework. Marcuse suggests a way out of this—autonomous thinking. In order to promote this, distance through privacy is advocated (so that we are not continually in contact with collective thought), as is interaction with art. Brookfield suggests that the only way to break free of one-dimensional thought is to "immerse adults fully and exclusively in a radically different perspective" (p. 215). Teaching critically, Brookfield proposes, is not only about how we teach, but also about what we teach. It is inherently political, and the goal is change. I would emphasize that we need to teach the questioning of all systems to be sure not to move from one form of one-dimensional thinking to another form of one-dimensional thinking.

What does this mean in terms of practice? Depending on the learning context, learner decision making may be encouraged by some of the following strategies:

- Using participatory planning in which students decide on some or all of the topics for a course, workshop, or other educational activity.

- Encouraging learners to suggest additional topics or substitute topics, to lead discussions, bring in resources, and otherwise participate in the ongoing development and modification of the sessions.

- Providing choices of methods, for example, suggesting that a topic could be dealt with in groups or in a large discussion or setting up the option of online discussion for those who prefer it.

- Giving students a decision-making model they can use as a guide to participatory planning and development or, alternatively, helping them develop such a model that is specific to the learning context.

- Suggesting that learners select and develop criteria for evaluation activities.

- Encouraging students to directly engage in self-evaluation where this is possible.

- Regularly asking learners for their perceptions of the learning experience and sharing one's own perception.

- Keeping the decision-making process open and explicit.

- Setting up teams or individuals who are responsible for some part of the decision making such as setting the agenda, forming groups, and coming to closure.

When learners make decisions or when some aspect of decision making has been delegated to the learner group, the educator cannot overturn the decisions arbitrarily. The educator remains accountable, however. If a decision seems inappropriate, the educator can discuss the problem with the learners and the group can reconsider the decision together. An interesting example of this process occurred this semester. In a course called Introduction to Educational Research that I am teaching online, I asked the participants, after two weeks of introductory material, to select the remaining topics for the course. They worked in participatory planning groups for a week and reported back to the discussion forum. I followed the planning discussions but did not intervene unless I was asked a direct question. The results were initially worrisome. None of the groups suggested any of the research methodologies (phenomenology, action research, grounded theory, and so forth) as topics. Instead, they expressed interest in how to read the research literature, how to critically analyze research, research ethics, applications of research in practice, and research issues of particular interest to their work as school teachers. How could I lead a course on research in education without including any of the research methods commonly used in educational research? As I discussed my concern with the group, I realized that for them, it was important to read, understand, critique, and apply research, but they were not and had no intention of becoming researchers themselves, so the details of how to use the various methodologies were of less concern. They were interested in seeing examples of different kinds of research, and they felt they would become familiar with methodologies through illustration and critique, but their primary goal was to work with material that would be relevant to their practice.

Considering Individual Differences

What is empowering for one person may not be for another. At the time of this writing, I am involved in planning the 2005 International Transformative Learning Conference with a group of colleagues. In a teleconferenced call, we were discussing possible keynote speakers, one of whom was described as being holistic and empowering through bringing body awareness to participants. One of my colleagues said, "I won't attend that one; some of us prefer to stay in our heads." Just as some individuals feel empowered through involvement in a discussion circle while others feel exposed and vulnerable, we all respond to power relations and empowerment strategies in different ways. In Chapter Five, I use psychological type theory to understand individual differences; I continue with this framework here and in the remaining chapters.

There are two commonsensical yet important ways to consider individual differences as we think about learner empowerment. One is to help learners develop an awareness of their own learning style, psychological type, values, and preferences. Understanding oneself is a component of critical self-reflection, so this serves two purposes—fostering self-awareness and empowering people to make decisions as to how they learn best. The second important strategy is for educators to develop an awareness of how learners vary in their preferences and to incorporate this awareness into everything we do. This does not mean that we need to develop four or eight or sixteen ways of doing everything, but rather that we are conscious of the variety of responses to what we do and how the same act on our part can lead to completely different reactions.

Learner self-awareness can be fostered informally or more systematically by using various inventories. Informally, a variety of activities can be used—values-based simulations, critical incidents, and role plays, for example—or simple discussion and questioning can help people become aware of their preferences. Most people know how they learn best and are interested in talking about it and sharing their experiences with others. Often the simple realization that there are others who share their inclinations for learning in a certain way is extremely helpful for students who might have felt alone or isolated in their preferences.

A variety of inventories can be used to measure psychological type and learning style preferences. The Myers-Briggs Type Indicator (Myers, 1985) may be the best known of the psychological type assessments. A colleague and I developed the PET (Personal Empowerment through Type) inventory (Cranton and Knoop, 1995), which yields a profile of preferences rather than a category or label. Among the learning styles inventories, Kolb's (1999) *Learning Style Inventory* remains popular in adult education. As with any such process, we must take care not to stereotype, label, or support people in using their learning preferences as a rationale for avoiding specific activities.

The educator who is conscious of individual differences will become aware of how this manifests itself in empowerment efforts. Trying to push an introverted learner to be "heard" in a discussion circle is disempowering, not empowering. Asking someone who is thoughtful and analytical to express deeply personal emotions may increase self-surveillance and even lead a student to invent things to please the teacher, but it will not feel empowering—quite the opposite. Refusing to provide structure or guidelines for a person who feels he needs this support, at least initially, will only exacerbate feelings of confusion and frustration. Encouraging someone who is extraverted and prefers to learn by doing to engage in quiet critical self-reflection or the contemplation of abstract and theoretical issues will similarly feel disempowering to the individual. This is not to say that we should continually, deliberately match our techniques to the expressed preferences of the learner—challenging people to develop their learning styles in new ways is important—but when empowerment is our goal, we need to work with people's preferences, not against them.

Summary

Although learner empowerment is often described as an outcome of transformative learning, I have argued here that people who feel powerless are less likely to engage in critical self-reflection. Empowerment is important to being able to embark on a transformative journey. An individual who is insecure, lacking in confidence, anxious, or unsupported may not be able to overcome the emotional barriers to questioning values and assumptions without first learning to exercise his or her power in relation to the teacher and other participants.

Educators can support learner empowerment in many ways, most of which exist in the small, ordinary, everyday interactions of the teaching and learning environment. We need to become conscious of power relations, including those that exist in the types of interactions we normally associate with democratic practice. Points of resistance are the other side of the power relations coin. We can watch for and examine students' and our own resistance to see where the power issues reside.

Given that power is exercised in all human interactions, educators need not only to become aware of where and how power relations exist, but also to exercise power responsibly. Sovereign power, that which is exercised from above by a person in a position of authority, is fairly easy to identify and avoid. Disciplinary power is less visible and more insidious, but educators can work to expose mechanisms of control and help adult learners recognize their own capacity to exercise power. So as not to lose sight of the good contributions of humanism in adult education, perhaps we can also name other power states: collaborative, empathetic, compassionate, shared, or just plain dancing.

Empowerment through discourse requires our careful attention. We must not fall into the trap of seeing discourse as an elitist endeavor that only the most articulate and educated of participants can enjoy. This is not the path to empowerment, at least not for those who are less articulate and have less formal education.

Learner decision making (self-direction, learner control, student autonomy) has a long history in adult education and may well be one of the central tenets of our practice, especially in the humanist and critical theory traditions. I briefly review the evolution of the concept and provide some practical suggestions for encouraging learner decision making as an empowering strategy.

It is essential that educators do not assume that all individual learners respond in the same way to empowering strategies. Individuals' values, learning styles, past experiences, and personality preferences contribute to how they will come to feel empowered and how they will respond to our efforts to help them on this journey.

8

Fostering Critical Self-Reflection and Self-Knowledge

The educator who has created an environment conducive to learner empowerment has set the stage for working toward transformative learning, but this does not ensure that learners will engage in critical self-reflection or revise their habits of mind. Essentially, an educator can do nothing to ensure that transformative learning takes place. Learners must decide to undergo the process themselves; otherwise, we are venturing into indoctrination, manipulation, and coercion. In a now classic article, Daloz (1988) describes how Gladys could not imagine, despite his efforts, alternative ways of approaching her job responsibilities. More recently, Lange (2004) discovers that for some of the participants in her study, the learning process could be better described as "restorative" than transformative, as they found their way back to important core values rather than revised their perspectives.

Still, we do not leave the possibility of students engaging in critical self-reflection, increasing self-knowledge, and potentially transforming perspectives to chance. It is our responsibility to help people articulate and examine beliefs and assumptions that have been previously assimilated without questioning, and there are many things we can do to foster this process. In the following two scenarios, the first educator helps Tammy feel comfortable but does not, at least initially, create an environment that leads to critical questioning, but the second educator sets Martin to thinking about his life.

Tammy grew up in a remote rural area of Tennessee and was the first in her family to complete high school. I was her neighbor at that time, and I shared in her joy. Tammy talked about her dream of going to college and becoming a nursing assistant. Getting to the nearest college involved driving "over the mountain," a forty-five-minute trip in good weather, and a treacherous one in the sometimes icy winter conditions. Tammy took a job in a local furniture factory with the goal of saving enough money to buy a car so she could get to the college. A few months later, she was laid off from her job, her parents were not well, and as Tammy stayed home to care for her parents and younger brother, the dream of the car and college became distant.

A couple of years later, when Tammy's family moved to town to be closer to the medical services they needed, Tammy nervously decided to go to college at last. I was able to stay in touch with Tammy and, I hope, provide some encouragement. She was assigned to an advisor who suggested she take courses called "College Orientation" and "Life Skills" as a part of her initial studies. Right away, Tammy could see that college was no place for her. Everyone was younger; the women all dressed so smartly; her Southern accent sounded foreign even to her own ears. But in her very first classes, people were so friendly and supportive. The teacher asked to be called by her first name; the students all sat in a circle and shared their fears; people could choose their own goals for the Life Skills course. Tammy chose to work on her accent, develop a study routine, and learn how to manage her time so that she could continue to help with her parents' care. It was not long at all before Tammy felt she was a part of the group and that she could succeed in college. I lost track of Tammy and am not sure how her experience developed from there, but it was clear her initial experiences did little to challenge her perspectives aside from her initial anxious response to being at college.

Martin grew up near a small town in southern Ontario's fruit-growing region. His father had immigrated to Canada when Martin was a baby and did what he knew best—he established a grape farm. Martin's father had never learned to read or write, but did not consider this to be especially important for a farmer. His vines were the straightest, his pruning the neatest, and his harvest the best in the area. Martin knew he would take over the farm one day, so he quit school as soon as he could do so legally and worked full-time with his father. He married young, and he and his wife built their own house next to a stream at the back of the largest grape field.

Life changed when the price of grapes fell to a third of their former value and the cost of fuel, insecticides, and fungicides skyrocketed. Neighbors were selling out; some were ripping out the vines and creating horse pastures. Martin decided to get some training in a trade so that he could supplement the farm income. He chose welding, as that would also be a useful skill to have around the farm.

Martin was shocked to find out that he was required to take "Life Skills" and "Communications." What did that have to do with welding? He had plenty of life skills already, whatever that meant. The Life Skills teacher turned out to be a woman who was younger than he. She had everyone sit in a circle, call her by her first name (and she a teacher!), and answer personal questions. Everyone had to tell their "life story" to someone else, and then the teacher asked rude questions about each story. "Why did you decide to do this?" "How do you think you'll be able to manage in school?" Everyone was uncomfortable. But Martin went home that afternoon wondering why he had never really considered finishing high school. What did education mean to him? Why was he just following in his father's footsteps? Couldn't a farmer also be a person who learned things? He and his wife spent the evening talking about what the teacher had asked and how it made Martin feel.

Uncomfortable questions can promote critical self-reflection if a learner is willing and ready to consider the questions. Martin's experience did that; Tammy's experience, on the other hand, was one of total support and comfort (which may well have later led her to change, but did not do so initially). Any strategy that opens up new perspectives, challenges existing assumptions, or presents information from a different point of view has the potential to encourage reflection and transformation. In this chapter, I present several such strategies: questioning, consciousness-raising experiences, journals, experiential learning, critical incidents, and arts-based activities.

Questioning

In their review of the first Conference on Transformative Learning, Wiessner and Mezirow (2000) list "Using Questions and Narrative" (p. 337) as one of the practical themes arising out of the conference presentations. Questions are effective, they suggest, in establishing an environment where people can figure out things for themselves, and questioning develops a constructive process appropriate for fostering transformative learning. Through thinking about and responding to questions, new avenues for understanding and new ways of seeing things are opened up.

Many general guidelines for asking good questions are given in the adult education literature. A few of these suggestions are

- Be specific—relate questions to specific events and situations.

- Move from the particular to the general.

- Be conversational.

- Avoid echoing students' responses to a question.

- Use follow-up questions or probes to encourage more specific responses.

- Do not ask questions that can be responded to in a simplistic, yes-no way.

- Ask questions that draw on learners' experiences and interests in relation to the topic.

Elsewhere, I developed a framework for asking questions in order to foster four types of learning: learning something new, elaborating on something known, transforming an assumption or belief, and transforming a broad perspective or worldview (Cranton, 2003). For the first two types of learning, I roughly follow Bloom's taxonomy in advocating memory questions, personalizing questions, application questions, analyzing questions, integrative questions, and evaluative questions. For the second two types of learning, I suggest content, process, premise, spiraling, and feeling questions. It is this latter set of questions that are relevant to fostering critical self-reflection and self-knowledge; I elaborate on these here. Content, process, and premise reflection are described more fully in Chapter Two.

Content reflection questions serve to raise learner awareness of assumptions and beliefs. In personal or psychological development (regarding psychological habits of mind), content questions take the form, *What do you know or believe about yourself?* The educator might ask, *What do you see as your skills in this area? What would you like to improve? What is your perception of yourself as a learner? What are you feeling about this decision?* or *What draws you to this area of study?*

On a social level (sociolinguistic habits of mind), content reflection questions take the generic form, *What are the social norms?* For example, the educator could ask, *What was the perception of this in your home community? What would be the feminist view on this issue? What views do the media present? What are politicians saying about this? What does the way we use language tell you about this area?* or *What would you say to this if you were the union leader?*

Content reflection can also be related to knowledge and the way we obtain knowledge (epistemic habits of mind), moral-ethical perspectives, philosophical views, and aesthetics (Mezirow, 2000). Educators can ask, for example, *What knowledge have you gained from your experience in this area? What does your conscience tell you? What religious or philosophical views inform your view?* and *What about this is beautiful?*

Process reflection questions address how a person has come to hold a certain perspective. If it is a problem being reflected on, process questions ask how the issue became a problem. Asking process questions helps learners find the source of an assumption or belief; sometimes it is useful to ask people whether they can recall a time when they did not hold a particular belief and then work forward from that time.

Examples of process reflection questions related to psychological habits of mind might be, *How did you come to see yourself this way? How did you choose this career? Can you recall how you came to hate statistics? How long have numbers made you feel anxious? Can you remember a time when you didn't feel this way? How was your view of yourself as a poor writer shaped?* Psychological beliefs are often uncritically assimilated in childhood, so process questions may be difficult to answer, and other strategies for fostering critical reflection may need to be used.

In the sociolinguistic area, process questions have the goal of unearthing the source of social norms that have been absorbed without thought. Again, norms absorbed in childhood can be quite hard to identify. Questions may take the form, *How did the community where you grew up influence that view? How did your experiences in high school shape what you believe? Has the media had an effect on what you believe? How does advertising influence your buying habits? Can you remember when you first encountered this point of view?*

Process reflection questions can also be asked of epistemic, moral-ethical perspectives, philosophical views, and aesthetics. For example, *How did you come to the conclusion that this theory is valid? Can you recall when you first adopted that stance? What led you to see this as unethical? How did you come to appreciate this style of photography?* and *How did you decide this research is flawed?*

Premise reflection questions get at the very core of our belief systems. They encourage the examination of the foundations of perspectives. Questions take the form of, *Why is this important in the first place?* and *Why should I care about this?* In the psychological arena, educators can ask, *Why does it matter that you are afraid of spiders?* or perhaps, *What are the consequences of your being afraid of spiders? How does this limit or constrain your life?* Care needs to be taken when asking premise questions about deeply held personal points of view; thinking about the issues can be emotional and traumatic. If I ask, *Why is your self-image of concern to you?* I could be unknowingly poking at the scar over a serious wound.

Premise questions in the sociolinguistic domain are the essence of critical theory. Ideology critique (ways in which people recognize uncritically assimilated and unjust dominant ideologies or sociocultural distortions) is one of the four traditions of criticality (Brookfield, 2005). Ideologies are embedded in our language, social norms, and cultural expectations. They are reified—they appear as givens and, as such, are difficult to dig out and examine. Hegemony is perpetuated through mass media images and messages, as well as social and institutional expectations and norms. People learn to live by the dominant system of beliefs.

We can ask, *Why do you value hard work? Why is it relevant what your extended family thinks? Why do you care about pleasing your boss? Why do you associate freedom with war? Why do we believe that it is only through education that people can come to engage in critical reflection?*

With regard to epistemic, moral-ethical, philosophical, and aesthetic habits of mind, premise questions take the same form but focus on a different kind of knowing. Educators could ask, *Why is that knowledge important? Why do we need to know that? Why does it matter if I behave ethically in that situation? What does understanding a philosophical stance contribute to anything? Why would we concern ourselves with the existence of God?* or *Why is art important in a person's life?*

To incorporate the recent movements to a more holistic understanding of transformative learning, I have added *spiraling* and *feeling* questions to the repertoire of critical questions we can consider using. Spiraling questions show how each part of what we know about who we are is related to every other thing we have learned and experienced. L. R. Cohen (1997) illustrates this process in his interactions with students who see themselves as not very smart. He does not ask just one question that leads his student to change the way he sees himself. He takes students back to what they know, what they can do, what they experience, and then asks a question that flips that perception around, then another question that connects back to the original perception but from another angle. In this way, a student who thinks he is stupid and a doctor is smart is led to see that he is smarter than the doctor when he can change a tire and the doctor cannot.

Feeling questions ask about spirit and body and call for imaginative perception in understanding constraints. When I teach carpenters and mechanics who are becoming teachers of carpentry and mechanics, they are changing everything about themselves, not just a cognitive perspective on their practice. Where do they put their pride in their working man's callused hands? What do they do with their feelings of superiority based on their being able to do physical tasks with ease? How do they deal with their friends' views of teachers as soft and lazy? How do they understand the sense of vocation that brought them to teaching?

Consciousness-Raising Experiences

Consciousness is a peculiar thing. It is an intermittent phenomenon. One-fifth or one-third or perhaps even one-half of human life is spent in an unconscious condition. The conscious mind moreover is characterized by a certain narrowness. It can hold only a few simultaneous contents at a given moment. All the rest is unconscious at the time, and we only get a sort of continuation or general understanding or awareness of a conscious world through the *succession* of conscious moments. . . . Consciousness is very much the product of perception and orientation in the *external* world. (Jung, 1968, pp. 6–8)

Consciousness-raising is breaking free from one-dimensional thought, understanding and unmasking power structures, recognizing hegemony, and critiquing social ideologies (Brookfield, 2005). Consciousness-raising occurs through exposure to different perspectives; acknowledgment of oppression; and critical, serious questioning of our own and others' beliefs. Through the writings of Freire (1970) and others, consciousness-raising has come to be associated with freedom from oppression; the term is also used in this way by feminist theorists. Individual or personal consciousness-raising as defined by Jung can be seen to form the basis of freedom from social oppression.

In some situations, consciousness-raising is promoted by exposure to new information, knowledge, insights, or values, especially those that are discrepant with our currently held points of view. But more commonly associated with consciousness-raising is seeing familiar things from a different perspective, thereby increasing one's self-awareness regarding familiar things.

Most people are fairly firmly entrenched in familiar roles—as professionals, as persons, and as learners. What happens once, we expect to happen again. We develop habits of mind, habitual expectations, and we make meaning based on these habits. Experiences that shake up these habits encourage critical reflection and expand self-knowledge. There are many kinds of learning activities that have this potential: role plays, critical debates, case studies, simulations, games, and life histories, to name a few. Whatever leads people to see something from a different point of view can act as a consciousness-raising activity. Here, I review a few such strategies.

Role play is one of the more common methods of helping others see things from a point of view outside of their normal perspective.

There are many variations on how role plays can be conducted. Generally, the purpose and context of the role play is described, and participants receive a description of the part they will play—usually not a script, but enough information that dialogue can be improvised. It is best if learners and educator collaborate on the scenario for the role play and integrate ideas from their experience and practice. Some people are uncomfortable with role plays, and although it can be good to challenge such discomfort, it is sometimes best to suggest that these individuals act as observers or reactors. Observers can watch for indicators of underlying, unconscious assumptions at play.

In order for role playing to lead to consciousness-raising, debriefing is important. Participants should have the opportunity to discuss their experience fully, especially what it felt like to view the situation from an alternative perspective. Videotaping may be helpful in looking for discrepancies between perceptions and behaviors.

Brookfield and Preskill (1999) present an interesting twist on the traditional role play in their description of conversational roles. Each participant has a specific conversational role to maintain: problem poser, reflective analyst, scrounger (listens for resources and tips), devil's advocate, detective (checks for unchallenged biases), theme spotter, and umpire (listens for judgmental comments). Other informal variations include

- Reversing roles in a discussion and presenting ideas from the other person's point of view

- Reversing roles that are played in real life (for example, a manager and a staff member, a union member and a manager)

- Participating in a discussion from the perspective of various authors or theorists

Consciousness-raising is initiated when the assumptions, values, and beliefs underlying the roles are made explicit and questioned.

Simulations can also be used to initiate awareness of alternative perspectives. Predesigned simulations are available from a variety of sources, but generally I find it more useful to create simulations related to the experiences of participants or the issues being addressed. In a graduate program Foundations Institute, participants had chosen to spend time learning about organizational change. My cofacilitator and I developed a simulation in which organizational teams designed proposals for a change in organizational structure and presented them to the board of directors. We called on our other colleagues to make up the board of directors and booked the boardroom in our building. Each team came in to make its presentation separately, and my colleagues, who became fully engaged in the role they were playing, asked challenging questions of each team.

In a gerontology group, participants can simulate the loss of hearing, eyesight, and tactile sensation by using earplugs, semitransparent blindfolds, and gloves and engaging in some routine activity. In a hospitality staff development session, a simulation of a hotel reception area can be set up with participants acting as clients, hotel staff, and managers. Whenever possible, people should be encouraged to take part in a simulation in a way that puts them in a position or take a stance they would not normally experience. In most subject areas, it is possible to set up interesting simulations that will help reveal values and beliefs and allow learners to see things from another point of view. As with any such strategy, it is important to leave a good amount of time for discussion and debriefing.

Just as narrative inquiry and self-study have gained popularity as research methodologies, *life story* and *autobiography* have become commonly used strategies for encouraging critical self-reflection and self-knowledge. Dominicé (2000) encourages the use of oral and written educational biographies as a way of understanding learners' frames of reference, their way of thinking about the world, and how this is embedded in cultural roots. Dominicé deliberately uses the phrase "educational biography," as he sees a person's life history as an educational process. He suggests that people both write and tell their story and present it to others in a small group in both formats. Group members interpret and reconstruct each other's biographies.

Life stories may also be focused on an aspect of learners' lives that is relevant to their area of study or interest. Johnson (2003) offers a model for integrating autobiography with any subject area. For example, I often encourage people to tell the story of how they became a teacher or an adult educator. In the Master's of Adult Education program where I currently practice, we open each new cohort group with a journey exercise in which individuals draw and then describe the journey that brought them to the program. In an English as a second language program, individuals could be asked to tell stories about their culture; in retraining workshops, participants could be invited to share their life story in relation to job choices and preferences. Most people enjoy telling stories and listening to others' stories. When the experiences of individuals in a group are diverse, the variety of perspectives in the stories naturally leads to awareness of alternatives and consciousness-raising. The educator should also actively draw out assumptions and values implicit in people's stories.

Journals

Journals and diaries have long been used as a means of self-expression. Writers, artists, philosophers, scientists, and researchers use journals to reflect on their life and work. Psychologists and psychoanalysts incorporate journal writing into their work with clients. Progoff (1992), who studied with Jung, has contributed extensively to the literature on journal writing. The Progoff journal process is presented at workshops and seminars across North America. He suggests a variety of formats and journal sections that may be helpful: a life history; a dialogue with a person from the writer's life or with a historical figure; a depth-dimension section containing metaphors, dreams, and images; and a life-study journal written from the perspective of another person.

Journals are now routinely used in a wide variety of subject areas and with different goals or purposes, ranging from a type of log or anecdotal record of what students have done to creative scrapbooks and Web-based blogs. In order to stimulate critical self-reflection and self-knowledge through journal writing, we need to emphasize the articulation of assumptions, thoughts, and feelings about issues and the consideration of alternatives. In my experience, the format or style of the journal does not matter a great deal; it seems to work best when people choose a format that they enjoy and are comfortable with. However, I sometimes provide suggestions or guidelines, especially when students seem to feel at a loss as to how to start.

- Divide each journal page in half vertically and use one side of the page for observations and descriptions and the other side for thoughts, feelings, related experiences, or images provoked by the description.

- Be assured that journals will not be checked for grammar or writing style or graded or judged in any way.

- Explore specific themes related to the course or program, such as "My thoughts on career options" or "My role as a professional" or "Past experiences that have influenced me."

- Establish a routine for journal writing—a time of day, a place, a special kind of book in which thoughts are recorded.

- Experiment with various styles and contents, such as writing to someone by using a letter format, recording dreams, working with poetry, or incorporating drawings with text.

As I mention in Chapter Seven, journals can be seen as a manifestation of disciplinary power. They are a way for the educator to "see inside of the mind" of the learner. We need to be conscious of this. No matter what we say, reading students' journals gives us access to their thoughts that we would not otherwise have. The process can lead to a situation where people write what they think the educator wants to hear or, worse, invent stories to demonstrate critical reflection or dramatic breakthroughs.

I suggest that no one should be required to write a journal, that no one should be required to give their journal to the educator, and that journals should not be graded by an educator. Some alternatives are (1) students can write a summary of their journal or choose excerpts to share with the educator, (2) dialogue journals can be used in which students write back and forth to each other, and (3) students can evaluate their own learning through keeping a journal. When we have the opportunity to read and comment on students' journals, our comments should be challenging and provocative but not judgmental. We should never contradict how the learner sees himself or herself, but we can question the origin of those perceptions and the consequences of holding them. Content, process, and premise reflection questions are useful (see the earlier section in this chapter on critical questioning). When I read journals, I tend to write many more questions in the margins than comments in other formats, though I am also conscious of indicating sections that I find insightful, interesting, and well-expressed.

Experiential Learning

Dewey's (1938) *Experience and Education* provides a strong foundation for the emphasis in adult education (and education in general) on experiential learning. Dewey (1933) also describes reflection through rational problem solving. Reflective thought is "active, persistent and careful consideration of any belief or supposed form of knowledge in the light of the grounds that support it and the further conclusion to which it tends" (p. 9). This sounds very much like what we hope for in encouraging critical reflection as a basis for transformative learning.

Kolb's (1984) experiential learning model is another historical marker of the importance of experience in learning. He describes learners as going through a cycle of concrete experience, reflection on that experience, abstract conceptualization, and application of the insights in a new context. Although people usually have a preference for one or more stages of the cycle, Kolb sees the complete cycle as comprising a meaningful learning experience.

In an online course on transformative learning that I am currently facilitating, participants have been discussing the transformative potential of moving from one culture to another and experiencing a very different lifestyle. It is often a new experience or new personal living arrangement that provokes the critical self-reflection that is a part of transformation. However, from the educator's perspective, there are innumerable ways to provide provocative experiences for learners, experiences that will challenge their way of seeing themselves or issues in the world around them. Practicums in professional education (nursing, teaching, dentistry, social work) and apprenticeships in the trades (carpentry, welding, auto mechanics, refrigeration) have long been used to help people come to see themselves in a new way—as a teacher, carpenter, and so on. On a smaller scale, any venture into the real world related to the area of study can be an eye-opening experience (for example, a visit to or volunteer work in an adult education center, attendance at or participation in the theater, a day spent working at a farm, participation in committees). The recent emphasis on service learning and job-shadowing demonstrates how educators in many fields are recognizing the importance of experiential activities.

Although the experience may, in itself, stimulate reflection, there are things that the educator can do to help this process along. Kolb (1984) emphasizes the importance of having opportunities to reflect on the experience: "The active/reflective dialectic . . . is one of *transformation*, representing two opposed ways of transforming that grasp our 'figurative representation' of experience—either through internal reflection, a process I will call *intention*, or active external manipulation of the external world, here called *extension*" (p. 41).

Some strategies that may foster transformative learning from experiential activities include

- Setting time aside both during and after the experience for critical discourse

- Suggesting that students write about the experience in a journal or in another format

- Encouraging critical questioning—for example, suggest learners develop a series of questions to ask each other

- Emphasizing any discrepancies between people's perceptions of the experience and theoretical positions

- Suggesting that learners share and compare other related experiences

- Brainstorming to generate insights, thoughts, and feelings derived from the experience

- Encouraging participants to develop plans for changes in their practice or personal life

- Validating new ideas in another experience

Critical Incidents

The critical incident technique was originally designed in the 1950s as a data collection method for qualitative research (Flanagan, 1954). People are asked to describe an incident related to a specific topic or theme—a time that stands out in their memory as being especially positive or negative. A set of questions designed to elicit details of the incident are asked, with the goal of determining what leads a person to interpret an experience as positive or negative.

Brookfield (1990, 1995) advocates critical incidents as a way of promoting critical reflection. The directions for a critical incident activity take the following general form:

- Think back over your last six months (or year) as a . . . (learner, teacher, worker, manager).

- Describe in about one-half page an event that was particularly positive (or negative) for you.

- Include when and where the incident occurred, who was involved, what was especially positive (or negative) about the incident, and what insights you gained from it.

The degree of structure and the number of questions addressed can vary. The ensuing discussion may be more important than completing the incident. Strategies I usually follow are

- Modeling a critical incident and encouraging students to question it

- Suggesting learners share their critical incident in pairs with people helping each other question the meaning of the incident

- Coaching learners to ask questions such as, *Why did you say this?* or *What led you to describe it in this way?* or *What would your colleague have said at this point?*

- Moving critical questioning from the specific to the general and from content to process reflection

- Asking for some examples of incidents in the full group but definitely not requiring everyone to participate

- Including some action planning in the discussion by asking, for example, *What would you have done differently?* or *What will you do next time in such a situation?*

- Ensuring that everyone feels their incidents have been addressed in some way and that there are no unnoticed emotional reactions

Brookfield has gone on to develop what he calls the Critical Incident Questionnaire (CIQ) (Brookfield, 1995; Brookfield and Preskill, 1999), a strategy for analyzing the learning process itself. Five questions are asked:

- At what moment in class this week were you most engaged as a learner?
- At what moment in class this week were you most distanced as a learner?
- What action that anyone in the room took this week did you find most affirming or helpful?
- What action that anyone in the room took this week did you find most puzzling or confusing?
- What surprised you the most about the class this week? (Brookfield and Preskill, 1999, pp. 49–50)

The educator makes note of themes among the responses and may include verbatim quotes to take back to the group for discussion. This modeling of critical analysis by the educator on his or her practice makes it easier for participants to engage in the same kind of analysis of their own ideas and beliefs.

Arts-Based Activities

Theorists who see transformative learning as an imaginative, intuitive process often advocate arts-based activities or the use of fiction, music, and art as stimuli for fostering transformation (Dirkx, 2001a, 2001b; Greene, 1995). Although we may worry about being "unacademic," especially in higher education (Shahjahan, 2004;

Tisdell, 2003), the move toward being more creative, innovative, and going outside the cognitive realm is certainly gaining momentum in adult education in general and perhaps especially among educators whose goal it is to foster transformative learning. The proliferation of arts-based sessions at the International Transformative Learning Conferences speaks to the interest of practitioners and theorists in this approach.

In my practice, I have encouraged students to venture away from the idea that essays are the only way to express learning with remarkable outcomes. The sculpture produced by a welding instructor, the quilt sewn by a new graduate student, and the paintings, music CDs, scrapbooks, and collages I have seen over the years demonstrate clearly how arts-based learning projects not only describe transformative learning but are transformative experiences in their creation. Here are some examples of learning projects or group activities that can be used:

- Bring in a variety of magazines and colored paper and scissors and glue sticks and have participants create a collage that represents the critical questioning of a social norm or an assumption in the field of study.

- In addition to, or instead of, the traditional essay or paper, encourage students to write fiction or poetry as a critique of a perspective or point of view.

- Give participants the option of representing the outcome of group work in a drawing rather than words.

- Encourage painting, sculpture, and music as ways of representing ideas.

- Use film, fiction, and photography to represent conflicting or alternative points of view on an issue.

- Write or put on a play as a group to demonstrate opposing ways of interpreting an event.

- Suggest a scrapbook or a series of photo collages as an alternative to a written reflective journal.

It is important for the educator to participate in learning activities proposed for students, and perhaps it is especially important with arts-based projects, where people are likely to feel more self-conscious or anxious about their ability to be creative. This point was brought back to me sharply in a recent online course. I had been neglecting participating in learning activities, which, online, are largely invisible to others in the group. One student asked me, "So what is your learning project?" I realized how beneficial my involvement was, and since I was experimenting with photography collages at that point, I decided to do one in relation to the course. I took great pleasure in creating the collage and even greater pleasure in posting it for students to comment on.

Individual Differences

By nature, some people are more likely to engage in critical self-reflection as a logical, analytical process than others. If we follow Mezirow's (2000) rational, cognitive model of reflection and transformation, people who have a preference for the thinking function are most likely to follow a process that is congruent with the theory. Other individuals, though, will respond well to experiential activities (those who prefer the sensing function) or to arts-based projects (those who are more intuitive by nature). Learners who have a preference for the feeling function may engage in group and relational learning activities more readily and comfortably than they would respond to the challenges of critical questioning.

In a recent discussion in my online course on transformative learning, participants proposed that people who tend to be introverted are more likely to integrate critical reflection into their daily activities, while people who lead extraverted lives need to consciously make time for reflection. In a study of dialogue in the online environment, a colleague and I saw good evidence of different styles and approaches to dialogue based on psychological type preferences (Lin and Cranton, 2004).

In fostering transformative learning, the educator must maintain an awareness of individual differences, consider which events will be more likely to lead to critical self-reflection and self-knowledge and in which learners, and expect variation in the processes that individuals go through. In an earlier work, I suggest strategies that may be useful for learners who have different psychological type preferences (Cranton, 2000a). I summarize those points here:

- Case studies, debates, critical questioning, and analyses of theoretical perspectives are of interest to learners who prefer the thinking function.

- Working together in pairs or groups to examine a frame of references is helpful for individuals who prefer the feeling function.

- Concrete, experiential strategies such as field trips and simulations can assist students who prefer the sensing function to explore alternative perspectives.

- Games, metaphors, imaging, brainstorming, and arts-based activities appeal to learners who prefer the intuitive function.

Summary

Critical self-reflection and self-knowledge is fostered when individuals encounter a point of view that is different from their own. In response to this discrepancy, people can ignore the new perspective, or they can be led to question the perspective they currently hold. As we go about our daily lives, we continually encounter values and assumptions that differ from our own. I think of reading, for example, letters to the editor in the local newspaper or listening to a national radio debate in Canada called "Cross Country Check Up" in which people express their opinions on issues important to our country. During these activities, I most often disregard or even feel superior to points of view that I disagree with. However, now and then, I am led to think about my own views in a critical way.

This is our job as educators—to come up with ways of creating that special moment when an individual thinks, "Oh, wait, let me reconsider this one." It can happen by chance, but we can also facilitate the process through carefully selected materials and activities. At the same time, we must keep in mind that it is *not* our job to impose points of view on others or to expect that everyone will rise to the challenges we present. It is often the case that, for a variety of reasons, people are not ready, willing, or able to make deep shifts in their habits of mind. But we still encourage reflection and hold open the possibility of transformation.

Critical questioning can be used to stimulate content, process, and premise reflection. These types of questions can lead people to make their assumptions explicit and to question the sources and consequences of their assumptions.

Consciousness-raising strategies increase self-awareness and involve looking at familiar things from a new perspective. Role plays, simulations, and life histories are useful activities for bringing things into consciousness.

Keeping a journal has a long history in adult education practice. When journals are used to encourage reflection rather than log events, they can be a powerful strategy for initiating transformative learning.

Thinking about and discussing critical incidents in participants' lives is an effective way of leading people from the specific to the general in understanding and challenging their assumptions and beliefs. A critical incident questionnaire can also be used to reflect on the process itself.

Arts-based activities provide an alternative to the traditional written word as a way of expressing beliefs and examining perspectives. As the interest in imaginative and intuitive transformation grows, practitioners are turning to creative and unusual ways to represent learners' journeys.

And, as in everything we do as educators, we must keep in mind that people are different. There will be no one strategy that will touch everyone, no one way that will clarify everything for every learner. Psychological type theory gives us one way of understanding these differences and selecting strategies that will be helpful to as many people as possible.

9

Supporting Transformative Learning

In transformative learning and emancipatory education, we recognize and work with discrepancies and distortions in the way we see the world. This can be a liberating and joyous process, but it can also have a dark side. Scott (1997) writes about the grieving involved in letting go of assumptions or values that have long been a foundation for our way of being in the world. Family and social life can be disrupted; people can feel lost and isolated. Daloz (2000) reminds us of the importance of a "climate of safety in which people feel free to speak their truth, where blaming and judging are minimal, where full participation is encouraged, where a premium is placed on mutual understanding, but also where evidence and arguments may be assessed objectively and assumptions surfaced openly" (p. 114). In discussing transformative learning for the common good, Daloz emphasizes the need to seek out supportive communities.

Belenky and Stanton (2000) argue that connected knowing is an alternative to communicative learning (which they subtitle "separate knowing"). Connected knowing "takes a radically different stance": "the more Connected Knowers disagree with another person the harder they will try to understand how that person could imagine such a thing, using empathy, imagination, and storytelling as tools for entering into another's frame of mind" (p. 87). From Belenky and Stanton's perspective, support is not something that is added on to the transformative experience, but rather it is an integral part of the process.

The educator who fosters transformative learning has a moral responsibility to provide and arrange for support. I do not mean that we need to become counselors or make a lifelong commitment to each individual we work with; however, we need to do everything we can to ensure that people are able to negotiate any difficulties they may encounter. Daloz asks, What *right* do we have to impose our values on our students? The stock answer to this is that we are not imposing our values but encouraging students to question their own, previously unquestioned values so that they may become more open to alternatives. But even here, we are, in a sense, imposing our value that it is better to become more open. Along with that imposition comes the serious obligation of making sure that people are all right.

I have worked with many students over the years whose lives have been turned upside down as a consequence, at least in part, of the kind of experiences they encountered in their studies. In Chapter Seven, I describe learner empowerment as a condition and an outcome of transformative learning; in Chapter Eight, I discuss ways of stimulating critical self-reflection and potentially transformative learning. I now turn to the significant role of support in the process. Being supportive of learners who are engaged in transformative experiences may not look very different from being supportive in any educational context. I am not sure that this matters. We do not know when and how transformative learning will take place in any one situation, or if it will take place, yet we keep it as a goal of our practice. Throughout our work, we strive to help people feel empowered, gain self-knowledge, and explore alternative ways of thinking, and we ensure there is support to balance these challenges. To varying degrees, the theorists integrate the role of support into their understanding of transformative learning. Mezirow (2000) mentions it briefly in relation to recognizing that the process is shared with others; authors such as Belenky and Stanton (2000) place relationships, support, and community at the center of their approach. Not everyone is comfortable becoming involved in students' lives; we each have our way of being supportive. I hope to provide enough variety in my suggestions that educators can find a way that is useful for them.

Following the thought that educators are different in the way they can be supportive, I first discuss how being authentic is central to being supportive. I then suggest strategies for building a group process that takes over some of the educators' functions. Learner networks outside of the classroom are another important source of support. Helping students understand and adapt to revised ways of thinking about themselves and the world is a part of what we must pay attention to, and in some circumstances, we can also assist people in planning a course of action based on their transformative experience. I devote sections of this chapter to each of these processes. Finally, I pay attention to conflict, ethical issues, and how people vary in their need for support.

Authenticity

In Chapter Six, I discuss authenticity in teaching as it relates to educator roles in general, and I describe research in which a colleague and I investigated this. Here, drawing in part on an overview of authenticity (Cranton, 2005a), I explore authenticity as it relates to supporting learners. Jarvis (1992) sees people as being authentic when they choose to act so as to "foster the growth and development of each other's being" (p. 113). Jarvis describes this as an experimental and creative act whereby adult educators consciously have the goal of helping another person develop. Teachers and students learn together through dialogue as Freire (1970) advocates. Brookfield (1990) also emphasizes building trust with students and respecting students as people.

Freire (1970) outlines six attitudes that need to be present for meaningful and authentic dialogue: (1) love for the world and human beings, (2) humility, (3) faith in people and their power to create and recreate, (4) trust, (5) hope that the dialogue will lead to meaning, and (6) critical thinking and the continuing transformation of reality.

Hollis (1998), a Jungian, integrates an understanding of persona (the masks we wear) with the importance of relationships in authenticity. The quality of relationships depends on how well we know ourselves and how authentically we bring ourselves to the relationship. Hollis proposes four principles of relationship: (1) what we do not know or want to accept about ourselves, we project onto others; (2) we project our wounds and longings onto others; (3) when the other person refuses responsibility for our wounds and longings, projection gives away to resentment and issues of power; and (4) the only way to heal a faltering relationship is to take personal responsibility for our own individuation.

Each of these perspectives emphasizes how authenticity is a part of relationship with others—as I suggest elsewhere, authenticity is the expression of the genuine self in a community or with others in relationship (Cranton, 2001). Buber (1961) believes that it is only through relationships with others that authenticity can be fostered. Being authentic in our relationship with students is central to being supportive. This is not to say that all teachers must have warm, deep, caring relationships with learners in order to be authentic or to be supportive. For some educators, a respectful distance is appropriate; for others, a collegial relationship; and for others still, a close relationship comes naturally (Cranton, 2003). What follows is a variety of suggestions for being supportive through different relationship styles (not all educators will be comfortable with all points):

- Demonstrate interest in and concern for student learning and development

- Share anecdotes from our own lives

- Establish shared professional or discipline-related goals with learners

- Illustrate and provide examples by drawing on our experience and encourage students to do the same

- Learn from our students while they learn from us

- Be accessible and encourage students to come to us outside of a class or session

- Refer to where we live, our children, pets, or hobbies in ordinary conversation

- Be receptive to helping students with problems and issues

- Follow up with students, asking whether they need help or are feeling comfortable

- Be there for learners in a way that is comfortable and open

Group Support

The educator is not the only one responsible for supporting learners in the process of transformative learning. In a cohesive learning group, people will be supportive of each other. Boyd (1989) emphasizes this when he writes that the learning group as a social system "can provide supportive structures that facilitate an individual's work in realizing personal transformation" (p. 467). In an effective, supportive group, there is

- Commitment to the group's goals

- Conformity to and protection of group norms

- Loyalty to the group

- Acceptance of responsibility within the group

- Good communication among group members

- Willingness to be influenced by group members

- Acceptance of others' opinions

- Willingness to endure frustration on behalf of
  the group

The group may be seen as a learning entity (Kasl and Elias, 2000) with the capacity to develop and transform. At the very least, the group can provide a protective and comforting blanket for those individual members who are experiencing the sad or difficult sides of transformation.

Not all groups emerge naturally into cohesive and supportive communities. Competition, conflict, power relations, and dominant voices are just a few of the many factors that can interfere with good group dynamics. How can we help students develop collaborative and supportive groups? Brookfield and Preskill (1999, pp. 9–18) list several dispositions of democratic discussion that I see as helpful:

- *Hospitality.* An atmosphere is established in which people feel invited to participate and in which there exists a mutual receptivity to new ideas and perspectives.

- *Participation.* A community is encouraged in which everyone can be involved in significant ways.

- *Mindfulness.* An environment is set up in which people pay close attention to one another's words, listen carefully and patiently to what others say.

- *Humility.* With humility, there is the willingness to admit that our knowledge and experience are limited and incomplete and that others can teach us something.

- *Mutuality.* It is in the interest of all to care about each other's self-development.

- *Deliberation*. The classroom is one where different points of view are presented and supported by evidence, data, and logic.

- *Appreciation*. People find the space and time to express their appreciation and gratitude toward each other, raising trust and bringing people closer together.

- *Hope*. We need to maintain the hope that we can reach new understanding, work through problems, and that pooling our talents can help us to do this.

- *Autonomy*. Individuals who are willing to take a strong stand and argue for it are important to a democratic community.

Brookfield and Preskill (1999) suggest that these group dispositions are ideals. It is helpful to name them openly and to model them in our educator roles within a group.

In writing about Carl Rogers's person-centered group process as transformative andragogy, O'Hara (2003) describes how groups evolve so as to support social learning. I incorporate some of her discoveries into my guidelines for encouraging group cohesiveness and support:

- Make the process of group development open and explicit—what is done and how it is done.

- Recognize the nonrational and emotional modes of consciousness in a group.

- Look for the universal in personal stories and for connectedness to the group and the subject under consideration.

- Strive toward open rather than rule-bound systems in group processes.

- Work toward accepting ambiguity and including those with whom we disagree.

- Have faith in the wisdom of the group over that of any one person.

- Suggest that the group act in a social role such as writing a letter of protest or applying for increased learning resources.

- Encourage the sharing of resources and expertise within the group.

- Meet as a group outside of the usual learning environment.

- Advocate doing learning projects in small groups, writing dialogue journals, or any activities that bring people together in their learning and development.

- Ask learners to solve group problems (conflict, coping with constraints, management issues) as a group.

Learner Networks

By learner network, I mean any sustained relationship among a group of people within a formal or informal learning context or a relationship that extends beyond the boundaries of the learning group. Within a learning group, small-group work, project teams, study partners, or peer teaching create networks that students can rely on when they need support and guidance. Outside of the learning group, people can become members of professional associations, clubs, self-help groups, and Internet discussion groups. Going on a retreat, attending a meditation center, taking up yoga, engaging in contemplative practices, or becoming a part of any common-interest activity can also provide support for an individual engaged in transformative learning, even though the activity may not be directly related to the content of the learning process. If we see transformative learning as being a deep shift in perspective, the whole of the self can be engaged; activities that foster mindfulness, peace, and quiet reflection in the presence of others can be valuable for some people.

Learner networks may form naturally just as supportiveness within a learner group may occur without any special effort on the part of the educator. And there may not be anything about the networks that is unique to transformative learning. Often, for example, small subgroups that work together in a course will remain in contact throughout a program or after they have gone on to different learning experiences. Nevertheless, we should not leave this important supportive process to chance. Some strategies that can be used to encourage the development of networks within a learner group are

- Using small-group activities or discussions during which learners can get to know each other and develop alliances

- Forming project groups or teams in which people work together over a longer period in an area of common interest

- Encouraging study partnerships or groups either informally or by setting up such groups as a part of the program

- Using peer teaching (participants sharing expertise with each other), jigsaw activities (each student or small group acquires expertise on one topic and then shares it with others), buzz groups (where students join together in small groups to address specific questions), or any other techniques for bringing people together

- Creating flexibility in meeting times for groups, teams, or pairs by giving up time from the regular schedule

- Fostering liaisons by referring learners to each other when they ask questions, share concerns, or encounter problems

We should also foster participation in networks outside of the learning group whenever this is possible or appropriate. I regularly make information available to students about relevant professional associations, conferences, and listservs. When people are engaged in a transformative process that is personal, it is important to be ready to make referrals to support groups, student services, or counseling services. Such services may be available through the institution in which we teach or, if not, through local community and social services. It is well worth making some phone calls to collect this information. We need to know when we cannot go any further in terms of providing personal support based on our knowledge of the person, the process, and our comfort level in the situation and then make the appropriate referrals. Sometimes, special interest groups are appropriate—for example, women's groups, international students' associations, or religion-based associations. It is easy and useful to help participants make contact with others who share their interests in a subject area or in personal development. I often recommend that a student contact another student whom I have worked with previously when I sense that they will be supportive for each other (with his or her permission, of course). Similarly, it can be valuable to refer learners to other educators or individuals in the community who have relevant interests or expertise. Finally, the ever-growing network of listservs, chat rooms, and other Internet connections can provide support for some people; this resource is especially useful for anyone who does not have easy access to face-to-face groups.

In addition to referring learners as individuals or as a group to outside networks, the educator can integrate this information into a course or workshop in a variety of ways. If we refer to our own involvement in professional or personal networks, our actions act as a model for students. In some cases, it is beneficial to ask learners to share their networking experiences with the group—people may have contacts that would be of interest to others. As a part of this discussion, educators can be explicit about the important role of networks in providing support. I also have included accessing networks as a part of a learning activity in a course; for example, I have suggested that participants go to a particular listserv and bring their reactions back to the group. When learners realize how much support is available through networking, they have a lifelong resource.

Help with Personal Adjustment

As I mention in the discussion of supportiveness through authenticity, educators need to make decisions about when and how they are willing to help learners with personal adjustment on an individual or situational basis. Each of us has a place where we feel comfortable and some, usually blurred, line where we begin to feel uncomfortable or out of our range of expertise. Educators regularly counsel students on job opportunities, courses or programs, thesis topics, project activities, and readings. Sometimes this advice can change a person's life. But we can be reluctant to step into what we perceive as being a student's *personal* life. Mezirow (1991) makes a helpful point when he writes that it is "necessary to make a careful distinction between adults who are having commonly encountered difficulties in dealing with familiar life transitions and those who have extreme neurotic, psychotic, or sociopathic disorders and require psychotherapy" (p. 205). It is reasonable to support the life transitions that come through transformative experiences, but, of course, it is dangerous and unethical to step in where professional counseling is needed.

I find that providing support through personal advisement further builds my relationship with students. It demonstrates my caring and develops trust; often, students engage in deeper critical self-reflection on the basis of open, caring support. As happens in any helping relationship, self-esteem and self-confidence may be increased and anxiety allayed by open dialogue. It is difficult to provide general guidelines for a process that is personal and individual. However, in his writings on mentoring, Daloz (1999) provides some helpful advice, and Griffin (2001), in her discussion of holistic learning and relationships with individuals, suggests some of the qualities teachers need to have. I draw on their ideas here, as well as on my own experience:

- Demonstrate empathy and positive unconditional regard for learners.

- As the relationship develops, help the student move away from dependency and into a collaborative role.

- Listen carefully and remain alert to things of special significance in what the individual says.

- Reinforce some elements of the student's story and let others slide by unacknowledged.

- Provide structure when it is needed—anxious students may want structure and guidance.

- Believe in your students; have positive expectations.

- Serve as an advocate for a student in the larger system or community if needed.

- Share things about yourself.

- Act as a mirror—mirror learners' comments and answers to enhance their and your understanding.

- Avoid giving opinions or advice; encourage individuals to find their own solutions through dialogue.

- Ask questions—open-ended questions, probing questions, reflective questions, and questions for more
  information.

- Help people distinguish realistic dangers from exaggerated fears.

Helping learners with personal adjustment usually takes place
in informal conversation. Going for a cup of tea or sitting casually at
a table in the office is more conducive to this kind of interaction
than is a classroom or more formal setting. Trust, respect, openness,
and genuine caring for the learner are key ingredients in providing
support and assistance for those who are struggling with a transformative experience.

Supporting Action

Each time I facilitate a course on transformative learning, the topic
comes up of whether or not action on the revised habits of mind are
a necessary part of transformation. Mezirow is quite clear on this.
He says that action is "an integral and indispensable component of
transformative learning" (1991, p. 209) and that the type of action
one takes "depends on the nature of the dilemma" (1997, p. 60).
Indeed, if transformative learning involves a deep shift in perspective, as is maintained by most writers in the field, it seems it would
be difficult not to act on such a change. Because people are different from each other, not everyone might go out and join protests or
try to make changes in an organization, but I would think that some
change in behavior would be evident. If we see the world differently,
we respond to it differently. Even the internal act of perception
makes for change. That change serves as action. And that internal
action will find expression in external actions. The educator has a
role in supporting actions arising out of transformative experiences.

One way of supporting actions is to help students learn to develop and implement action plans. It is one thing for a learner to

say, "I now see the role of women in organizations in a completely new way," and it is something else for that learner to discuss this view with a hostile colleague, change her behavior at work, join a fight for pay equity, establish a committee to investigate women's issues in her own organization, or take a role in a national feminist group. If a person knows how to plan action based on a new perspective, such steps may not be so formidable.

Often the educator is with learners for a restricted period, and the action takes place after learners have left the educational setting. The skill of independently planning action can be used in any setting at any time. The very idea of action planning is a cognitive, rational one, but I try to incorporate more imaginative and relational aspects into the following strategy:

- *Set a goal or create a vision.* Actions do not even need to be observable to others. Some examples include make a decision to do this, write about that in my journal, discuss this with my wife, write a memo to my boss on this issue, or share my vision with my colleagues.

- *Think about tomorrow and think about next year.* A short-term goal may be to discuss the new ideas with someone at work, but what does this mean in the long term? What will the learner do next year or in five years from now that could reflect the changed perspective?

- *Consider boundaries and resources.* It may be important to bear in mind a time frame within which a goal will be worked toward and to consider the people who will be affected. The world cannot be changed tomorrow, and not everyone will be wildly supportive if the change is dramatic. Other considerations might include resources required, financial issues, expertise needed, or practical constraints.

- *Imagine alternatives, options, and consequences.* A part of developing critical thinking, as outlined by Brookfield (1991), is imagining alternatives, and I think this comes into play as well in supporting action. We need to help the learner imagine and think about alternatives, options, and perhaps especially the consequences of change.

- *Implement.* Sometimes having a goal is not enough— we need to think about what we will do in concrete terms to act on a change in our lives. Here, the educator can help the learner by discussing ideas and offering suggestions.

- *Ask for feedback.* Transformative changes in people's lives often influence others. When this occurs in the workplace, it might be helpful to encourage learners to ask others for feedback on any changes that might be visible to them. This could be done informally or in a more structured way.

Conflict and Ethical Issues

In the movie *Mona Lisa Smile*, Katherine, the educator, challenges her students to move beyond the 1950s' social norms that guide their lives. When her student Joan decides to marry rather than go to law school, and Katherine objects, Joan challenges Katherine's right to tell her how to live. In another exchange, a conflict in values with ethical implications is clear:

BETTY (student): Don't disregard our traditions just because you're subversive.

KATHERINE (teacher): Don't disrespect this class just because you're married.

BETTY: Don't disrespect me just because you're not.

As Merriam and Caffarella (1999) say so well, "Most educators believe in the 'goodness' of continued learning—that more is better than less, that through education both individuals and society can advance to higher levels of development. But what of the unintended outcomes of learning. . .? What responsibility do we have for the pain and discomfort of our learners as well as their growth and successes?" (p. 383). Our modernistic assumption that growth is always good and to be cultivated leaves some questions unanswered.

At both the social and the individual levels, transformative learning is fraught with such ethical questions. When people become aware of their oppression and take action to change their situation, they are not only making changes in their own lives but in the social structure that allows the oppression to exist. This is a political and possibly an economic process that could, in some situations, lead to violence or further disadvantaging of certain groups. In the spirit of Freire, Nesbit (2004) reminds us that "education and teaching are profoundly political" (p. 17) and that attempts to advance the values of our own social class in our teaching are quite political.

At the individual level, the consequences of teaching for empowerment are no less profound. Mezirow (1991) writes, "The educator's objective should be only that the learner learns freely and decides, on the basis of the best information available, whether or not to act and, if so, how and when" (p. 203). He goes on to say that "to avoid the question of values is to opt for perpetuating the unexamined values of the status quo" (p. 203), a sentiment that Brookfield (2005, for example) often expresses, and one that Nesbit (2004) implies when he argues that educational systems reproduce the social relations required for capitalist production. However, the assumption underlying these points of view is that the ultimate educational achievement is to continuously critically question our values and assumptions and those we see in the world around us. I believe this too but in a slightly nuanced way. Although I find it virtually impossible to argue against the educational goals of empowering the oppressed and addressing inequalities and injustices inherent in social structures, it is the idolization of the critical mind that causes me to ponder the ethical issues involved in doing so. Or perhaps it is the devaluing of concepts such as faith, conviction, and trust that is a concern. In our practitioner roles, I think we need to be diligent in asking ourselves, *What right do I have to encourage you to question what you believe? When is it a responsibility, and when is it an imposition? When is it empowering, and when is it destructive? At what point do I need to leave aside my ego and thirst for learners to do as I do?*

The power relations that exist between educator and learner underline the necessity for sensitivity. A student may be influenced by an educator's values in ways that he or she would not be influenced by a peer. Usually this influence is positive; most educators are moral and good people. But even so, cultural, gender, and social differences between the educator and the student can lead to elusive ethical dilemmas and conflicts. As Smith (2004) points out, members of the dominant group are often unconscious and unaware of their privilege, and unable to recognize their power and prejudice. Marginality is embedded in individual and institutional attitudes. Smith's example of being mistaken for a waiter at a workshop based on his being African American certainly makes this point clear. Recently, I caught myself assuming that the author of an article was female because the content was emotionality in learning. None of us is immune from these stereotypes given the culture we live in.

When making their values explicit, educators should always include alternatives and model questioning of their own values. Similarly, educators must respect the values of learners even while encouraging questioning of them. Perhaps most important, educators should reflect continually on their practice, examining the influence they have on learners and questioning the nature of that influence. Anything less fails to provide support and may be unethical.

There may be occasions when, through critical self-reflection, a student makes choices with which the educator is politically, culturally, or morally in disagreement. Mezirow (1991) suggests that as long as there is agreement in the group that everyone's interpretation is open to questioning, there is no reason for the educator to have reservations about continuing the process. However, if someone chooses a course of action that the educator cannot accept, he or she should withdraw, or, if the choice is potentially harmful, the educator should intervene. This very awkward and difficult situation is not one that I have personally experienced, and I imagine it occurs rarely. In most circumstances, I think the educator would be able to be open about his or her position and continue to work with the person. Supporting learners who are working toward transformative learning involves managing conflict and living with ethical issues in a responsible, professional, and open manner.

Individual Differences

Supporting transformative learning requires a good understanding of individual differences in style, psychological preferences, values, culture, race, and gender. Brookfield (2005) includes two valuable chapters in his book on critical theory—one on racializing criticality and another on gendering criticality. In our efforts to support transformation, we need to be conscious of not only a person's preferred individual style, but, as much as possible, that person's social context. Raciality, ethnicity, and gender are a part of the personal and social being—they constitute the experience of being in the world and inform a person's worldview.

Educators are not superhumans; we can only look at the world through our own eyes along with everyone else. In being supportive of transformation, we need to rely on our relationship with learners and the trust, respect, and openness we build with people. The following case is based in part on a student's dialogue journal, but it is also a compilation of several experiences.

Originally from China, Chen has been in North America for several years. His psychological type preference is for extraverted sensing, but he does not have a clear secondary preference. Chen questions the cultural biases of the instrument and describes his home culture as valuing thinking to the exclusion of feeling. He suggests that this has influenced his responses to many of the items on the inventory. The educator is a Canadian white woman about the same age as the student. She has a limited knowledge of Chinese culture. Her psychological type preferences are for introverted thinking and introverted intuition. The educator and Chen meet in a formal credit graduate course in adult education and then continue to work together on an independent study.

Initially, Chen wanted to accumulate as much information as possible and expressed frustration in his journal when the educator did not provide the information he was looking for. He also questioned the value of writing a journal, wrote very short entries, and said he did not know what to write about. The educator consistently expressed her belief in the value of journal writing and commented that learning was much more than the accumulation of facts. Both student and teacher were frustrated. Hostility was apparent in some of the journal entries, and humor was used to disguise some of the hostility.

There was no group of learners meeting regularly at this time, and the educator was not only trying to fix the communication problem herself but was also assuming full responsibility for it. Finally, there was a turning point. The educator wrote, "I suggest that you discuss this with Ric; I know he has collected information on that topic." The next journal entries were longer, and surprisingly, Chen seemed to pay less attention to acquiring information, even though this was what the educator had used to connect with him in her comment. Chen reports on his discussion with Ric. He wrote, "In my background, the teacher was always the source of all information," and later, "Ric agreed that he also expected the teacher to know everything, and he has trouble with this too." A bit later, Chen wrote, "I see it as immoral that you try to change me to be like you." The educator responded that her only intention was to encourage questioning and that she agreed it would be wrong to try to change someone. Chen took the educator's comment at face value and responded, "I'm so glad you agree with me. So, why do you question the information I give you?" This issue was not resolved.

Chen's psychological type preference should have led him to an interest in action based on his learning (which he did describe as transformative), but when asked about the practical implications of his learning or what he would now do, he ignored the questions. Eventually, he began to see how his experience would relate to his goal of teaching English as a second language, and he applied this to his thesis.

Although the educator had a good understanding of psychological type theory, she had a limited understanding of Chen's culture, and this made it hard for her to be supportive of Chen's development. Referring Chen to another student for support seemed to be the turning point in the story. When an educator works with a learner whom he or she truly cannot understand, it is important to involve others in being supportive.

Summary

Transformative learning, the process of developing more open and better justified habits of mind, frees people from constraints and is a liberating experience. But in the journey there can be times of grief, pain, conflict, and a feeling of loss of the old way of life. The educator who helps initiate this journey is responsible for ensuring that support is available. Support comes through relationship with another person and especially through relationship with someone who is authentic, open, and genuine in their caring. Becoming an authentic teacher is, in itself, an important developmental and transformative process for the educator, and making that explicit helps establish trust and support. Each educator needs to find his or her own best way to form relationships with learners.

Learners often turn to their peers for support, especially when they are able to identify with others who are going through a similar experience. It is not up to the educator to be everything to everyone. Establishing a good, warm, and helpful group can be critical in supporting transformative learning. As Taylor, Marienau, and Fiddler (2000) suggest, changing *how* one knows includes a dimension of connectedness with others: experiencing oneself as a part of something larger, contributing one's voice to a collective endeavor, and recognizing that collective awareness and thinking transform the sum of their parts.

Networks that form within a group as well as those that stretch outside of the learning group are another source of support for people engaged in a transformative process. Learner networks can be based on shared personal or professional interests, and they can take the format of study groups, Web-based listservs, or professional meetings.

Transformative experiences can lead to many changes in a person's life, some of which are difficult, personal, and hard to integrate into the fabric of being. Students may turn to the educator who set them on this path for help when things are going badly. Personal advisement is not something every educator is comfortable doing; each person needs to work within the boundaries that feel right in the particular relationship with the student and be ready to refer someone for another kind of help if that seems appropriate. I discuss some general guidelines for helping people with personal adjustment.

Another part of supporting transformative learning is helping people act on their revised habits of mind. Often, students have already left us when they come to the point of basing actions on their learning, but we can help people prepare for that stage by planning for action with them. This is a skill that will be useful throughout a learner's life.

The very nature of transformative learning raises ethical issues. Transformation can lead to conflict in a person's life—within the family, community, and culture. Moving out from under constraints or oppressive states calls into question that which led to the oppression in the first place, and that can be anything from a person's own family through to complex social and power structures. Educators need to be conscious of the potential conflicts and the related ethical issues.

And finally, people vary in their individual styles, values, and preferences, as well as in the social context that shapes who they are. Being supportive is based on a connection with a whole person. Being aware of and sensitive to the individual and the context that has shaped that person is essential in that process.

10

The Educator's Transformative Journey

Since the publication of the first edition of this book, I went on to write *Professional Development as Transformative Learning* (Cranton, 1996) in which I examined in detail how adult educators engage in critical reflection on their practice, leading to transformative learning about teaching. During the same time frame, Brookfield (1995) wrote *Becoming a Critically Reflective Teacher*, an analysis and guide for educators who are working to become more reflective in their work. I have since come to view becoming authentic as a transformative process for educators (Cranton, 2001) and have carried out research to understand this more fully (Cranton and Carusetta, 2004b). Developing a philosophy of education is now a fairly standard practice. In her thoughtful analysis of the role of transformative learning in higher education, Moore (2005) describes how she is attempting to break free from institutional norms and barriers and in doing so she writes, "I am simultaneously experiencing transformations on a series of conscious and unconscious levels" (p. 89).

Although we now pay more attention to how adult educators learn about teaching than we did in the past, it is still not common to talk about it as potentially transformative. At the annual meeting of the Professional and Organizational Development (POD) network—an association dedicated to educator development—the focus is more often than not on the acquisition of specific skills and techniques rather than on critical self-reflection (Cranton, 2005b).

Using transformative learning theory to understand learning about teaching, we find that in order to expand the habit of mind related to "being an educator" we might experience the following: increasing self-awareness through consciousness-raising activities, making our assumptions and beliefs about our practice explicit, engaging in critical reflection on those assumptions or more intuitively imagining alternatives, engaging in dialogue with others, and developing an informed theory of practice (or a better justified perspective on practice). When we achieve new growth in our personal development, we also spontaneously achieve increased self-awareness, which we bring into our professional development.

The acquisition of technical knowledge about teaching cannot be overlooked, but it would be informed by a broader-based sociolinguistic, psychological, moral, aesthetic, and philosophical base. That is, technique should not drive an educator's perspective of practice; rather a perspective of practice should determine what technical knowledge is required. When I ventured into the exciting world of online teaching and learning, I gathered technical skills as I realized what I needed to know in order to create the kind of learning community I wanted to have.

In this chapter, I follow transformative learning theory to talk about how we can engage in a meaningful developmental journey. It is my intent to provide suggestions that each educator can consider, try on, reject, or elaborate on in order to find his or her path. If we are to foster transformative learning among our students, it is important that we experience and model the process ourselves, and what better forum than in professional development?

Awareness of Self as Educator

Most of us do not stop and think about who we are as an educator. We are rushing from task to task, planning tomorrow's workshop, giving feedback to students, and meeting our many responsibilities in our personal and professional lives. It is easier to base our decisions about practice on what we have done before that has worked or on what we have seen or heard others do. In Chapters Six and Nine, I suggest that communication and relationships with students are founded on authenticity, bringing one's sense of self into teaching practice. This means that self-awareness is an important building block for good teaching. Self-awareness also provides the groundwork for transformative learning about teaching.

Activities such as keeping a teaching journal, setting up a teaching discussion group with colleagues, taking a workshop on reflective teaching, reading inspirational books on teaching (for example, Apps [1996] or Palmer [1998]), or completing an inventory on psychological type preferences or learning style (for example, Cranton and Knoop [1995] or Kolb [1999]) are all useful ways of developing awareness of yourself as a teacher. Here, I suggest questions to consider for self-awareness in three domains: psychological, sociolinguistic, and epistemic (knowledge about teaching).

Psychological perspectives, as I discuss in Chapter Two, have to do with how people see themselves—their self-concept, needs, inhibitions, anxieties, and fears. Questions we might ask ourselves include

- What ten words might I use to describe myself as an educator?

- What values do I hold in my personal life that inform my teaching?

- How would I describe my confidence or self-concept as an educator?

- How is my self-concept as an educator similar to or different from how I think of myself outside of teaching?

- Do I feel I have personal control in my practice?

- What do I like and dislike about being an educator?

- What personal needs does being an educator fulfill?

- How does my personality suit or not suit my being an educator?

- What inhibitions or fears do I have in relation to my work?

Sociolinguistic habits of mind are based on social norms, cultural expectations, and the way we use language. Many of the ways in which we see ourselves as educators come from the social construction of what it means to be an educator. Some questions to consider are:

- How do people in my community see educators?

- How do the media describe educators?

- Was my decision to become an educator influenced by my family, community, or culture?

- What social role should an educator have outside of his or her practice?

- How does society script or determine educator roles? How do films and television representations influence this?

- What language is used to talk about educators' work?

- Do people treat me differently when they know I am an educator? How?

- What do my students think an educator should be like?

- What are my organization's or institution's expectations of educators?

Epistemic habits of mind are those related to knowledge and the way we acquire and use knowledge. What we know about teaching and how we learn about teaching determine, at least in part, how we see ourselves as teachers. I suggest reflection on the following questions:

- Where and how did I gain my knowledge about teaching?

- How would I describe my learning style and teaching style?

- What is the most important thing for a teacher to know?

- What is my philosophy of practice?

- How much do I know about being an educator?

- What would I like to learn about teaching?

- Am I a good teacher?

- What do others—students, colleagues, friends—say about my teaching?

- Do I always want to be a teacher?

- What is it about teaching that is most interesting?

Describing and questioning our perspectives on our practice helps increase self-awareness and sets the stage for a more comprehensive consideration of assumptions and beliefs about being an educator.

Palmer (2004) reminds us that the path of increased self-awareness is not "onward and upward," but rather "up and down and back and around" (p. 90). Sometimes autobiographical details are too painful to be talked about openly, and Palmer suggests exploration through poetry, story, music, or art—"any metaphorical embodiment that allows us to approach the topic indirectly" (p. 90). He also emphasizes asking honest, open questions of each other—questions that invite the "soul to speak" rather than represent the views of the person asking the question.

Revealing Assumptions

A colleague recently asked me what metaphor I would use to describe my teaching. The question drew me up short for a moment. It is the kind of question I would ask my students, but I had never really thought about it in relation to my own practice. I described a favorite photograph of mine—one of clear water running over colored rocks of various sizes—and then thought about what assumptions this metaphor might reveal. I want my practice to be clear, transparent, and fluid. My work runs through, around, over, and under the learning environment. Each individual rock (participant) is a different color, shape, and size. The water brings out the color and accentuates the differences among the rocks. Our assumptions are deeply embedded; they come from early experience, from our community and culture, and from what we know about the world. It is hard to step outside of our own point of view and isolate unarticulated and uncritically assimilated assumptions. This is as true for us as educators as it is for the people whose transformative experiences we are fostering.

Brookfield (1995) suggests we need others to hold up a mirror to help us see our assumptions. But this can be a frightening experience: "We wear an external mask of control, but beneath it we know that really we are frail figures. . . . Around the corner is an unforeseen but cataclysmic event that will reveal us as frauds" (p. 230). We ask our students to unearth their hidden assumptions about a variety of things in sometimes quite personal arenas; we need to do the same. Any of the activities described in Chapter Eight can be used for helping us articulate our own assumptions. In addition, I especially like two strategies Brookfield (1991) describes: *criteria analysis* and *crisis-decision simulations*.

Criteria analysis comprises three parts: the educator imagines or describes a specific situation in which success or failure in practice has occurred. The standards used to determine the success or failure of the situation are made explicit, and indicators of those criteria are identified. Two possible scenarios are

- Imagine that you are a professional development consultant who has been asked to observe and provide feedback on a colleague's practice. What features would you be looking for as evidence that this educator is effective?

- Imagine that one of your colleagues has recently been accused of poor teaching and professional negligence. You have been given the task of serving on a committee to establish a code of conduct for educators in your institution. What indicators would you choose as evidence that someone was behaving in a professional manner?

The scenarios ask the educator to think about what good teaching or good professional practice is. The responses can then be used to uncover assumptions. Suppose I said, in response to the first scenario:

I would look for subject-area knowledge and expertise. I would be interested in a dynamic and enthusiastic presentation, one that would stimulate enthusiasm among the students. But perhaps, most important, I would check for a well-organized presentation in which the educator made her expectations clear and everyone knew what was coming.

What assumptions would I be making? I may not be aware of them—they would have come from my past experience, my personal preferences, and probably the social construction of good teaching.

Through reflection or dialogue with others or both, I might realize I was making the following assumptions: (1) an effective educator is an expert, (2) an enthusiastic teacher makes enthusiastic learners, (3) good teaching means having an organized presentation, and (4) learners prefer to be told what to do.

The crisis-decision simulation is similar, but a bit more dramatic. Here, people are asked to imagine a situation where they must make a decision among several uncomfortable choices. An example scenario is

Imagine that you are on a committee required to make a decision about which courses in your program will be cut due to severe budget restraints. You have to eliminate two of the following: a workshop series on the new spreadsheet system for support staff; an advanced seminar in Web construction for computer technicians in the organization; or an online course on action learning for the senior managers.

The content of the scenario can obviously be adjusted to best suit the educator's context. Discussion of the choices should include speculation about the rationale for the decision and feelings experienced in making the decision. Making difficult choices often helps reveal underlying assumptions and values.

The scenario-based activities and the ensuing discussion are primarily cognitively-based strategies. As I illustrate with my metaphor example, more imaginative approaches are likely to be valuable for many educators. Dirkx (1997, 2000) emphasizes this in his understanding of transformative learning theory. Greene (1995) passionately advocates the use of the arts as a tool for helping us imagine the realities of worlds other than our own. Palmer (2004) writes about using a "third thing" (a poem, a story) as a way of exploring inner issues as we project our needs onto the story. Film, art work, fiction, poetry, and photography can be used to stimulate discussion of beliefs about teaching. How are teachers portrayed in films and fiction? What poem symbolizes something about teaching? If you were to represent the qualities of good teaching in a painting, what would you paint?

Critically Questioning and Imagining

Content, process, and premise reflection, as described in Chapter Two, provide an interesting framework for educators questioning their assumptions and beliefs about their practice. Keeping a teaching journal and discussing teaching with colleagues can form the basis for reflection. I often send my teaching journal to a trusted colleague; he replies with comments, support, and good, critical questions about what I have written. I have sometimes shared excerpts from my teaching journal with students to obtain their reactions and insights about an issue I am struggling with. I regularly ask learners for comments on our courses both in writing and in open discussions. All of these sources feed into my consideration of:

- What did I do in that class, session, or workshop? (content reflection)

- How did I come to do that? (process reflection)

- Why is this important to me? (premise reflection)

Experimentation with practice also creates a good way of questioning, reflecting, and imagining alternatives. This can be as simple as trying a new method and observing and speculating on the results or as complex as designing an action research project (see Kuhne and Quigley, 1997, for example) to systematically investigate a specific question.

Kegan (2000) beautifully illustrates the process of rejecting one's identification with uncritically assimilated assumptions by quoting Nora's speech in the closing scene of Ibsen's *A Doll House*. As Kegan suggests, critically questioning and imagining is not simply about coming to new ideas, but rather coming to "a new set of ideas about . . . ideas, about where they even come from, about who authorizes them or makes them true" (p. 57).

Consultation with professional development consultants or a human resource person can provide another perspective on our work and encourage critical reflection. Consultations take several different formats: ongoing discussion, observations of teaching, videotaping of sessions, workshops, and readings. Even if a workshop is advertised as a how-to-do-it session, it can give us an alternative way of thinking about our practice if we approach it with that mindset.

Essentially, any activity that encourages us to think about our teaching from a different angle or to imagine teaching in a different way is helpful. Some additional ideas are

- Read a book from a point of view that is different from our own (for example, a book on presentation skills if we normally facilitate group process)

- Observe a colleague who has a different style from our own

- Exchange teaching journals with a colleague

- Read about research on teaching

- Work with a "critical friend" and ask each other questions about practice

- Create a drawing that depicts our practice and one that depicts how we do not practice

- Read novels about teaching and learning

- Look at all of our experiences of art and literature to see what they tell us about teaching and learning

Palmer (2004) writes about "approaching soul truth 'on the slant' through the use of third things" in a "circle of trust" with others (p. 114). Novels and drawings are "third things" that can lead us to see ourselves more clearly, especially through open, honest, and trusting dialogue with others.

Engaging Others in Dialogue

Dialogue has already come up in each of the preceding sections on self-awareness, articulating assumptions, and critical reflection, but it is important enough to elaborate on here. Educators, especially in more formal settings, tend not to discuss their teaching with their peers. Adult educators are often working in isolation from others; much of the work is part-time, at night, or peripheral to the organization. In their integrative chapter on searching for the common ground in transformative learning theory, Wiessner and Mezirow (2000) describe "talking" as one of the themes: "Once space is created for transformative learning, ways of listening and speaking within that space become important" (p. 336). Whether it is Belenky and Stanton's (2000) full-circle conversation, Kegan's (2000) "discourse of inner contractions" and "developmental discourse," Palmer's (2004) "circle of trust," or Mezirow's (2000) description of empathic listening in discourse, dialogue plays an important role. Wiessner and Mezirow (2000) also list the use of questions and narrative as a common interest across a variety of approaches to transformative learning. We know the value of dialogue in our work with learners; we need to recognize the necessity of dialogue about teaching as a means of fostering our own development.

In order to engage in dialogue with others with a view to transformative learning about teaching, some of the following suggestions may be of use:

- Initiating discussion groups that meet regularly to discuss participants' practice or specific themes related to practice

- Creating a discussion group to review and question books about teaching in adult education

- Establishing a group of critical friends who meet to help participants challenge their frames of reference about teaching

- Joining one or more listservs related to teaching (for example, the Professional and Organizational Development, the Society for Teaching and Learning in Higher Education, or the Commission of Professors of Adult Education listservs)

- Participating in conferences, such as the Adult Education Research Conference, the International Transformative Learning Conference, or the Canadian Association for Studies in Adult Education Conference

Transformation must come from within. Feeling coerced into following someone else's advice may lead to short-lived changes, but not to deep and abiding shifts in perspective. Palmer (2004) follows a simple rule in his facilitation of circles of trust: "No fixing, no saving, no advising, no setting each other straight" (p. 115). He suggests that our habit of advising each other reveals its shadow side, saying something like, "If you take my advice, you will surely solve your problem. If you take my advice but fail to solve your problem, you did not try hard enough. If you fail to take my advice, I did the best I could. So I am covered. No matter how things come out, I no longer need to worry about you or our vexing problem" (p. 117). Our goal in engaging others in dialogue should not be to be fixed or saved, but rather to be seen and heard. Palmer says that the best service he can provide is to hold the speaker in a space where he or she can listen to the inner teacher.

Describing a Perspective on Education

Whether we call it a theory of practice, a philosophy of practice, or a perspective on education, we need to have a rationale or a mission or vision for our teaching. What do we believe about education? What drives us to do our best? What do we hope to achieve? I have followed Brookfield's (1995, 2005) thinking about teaching as a political activity (see Chapters Seven and Nine); even if an educator sees herself as remaining neutral, she is thereby supporting the status quo, which is, in itself, a political stance. Choosing content or strategies for facilitating a group always has an underlying meaning, whether we make it conscious or not. Naming and describing our frame of reference about education and our role within that world is a part of our transformative journey as an educator.

Brookfield (1991) suggests that a philosophy of practice should include at least three elements: a clear definition of the activity concerned, a number of general purposes for the field derived from this definition, and a set of criteria by which the success of the educator's work can be judged. The three questions we can ask ourselves are:

- What is my definition of an adult educator?

- What are the purposes of adult education in my field?

- What do I do to work toward these goals, and how successful am I?

These questions can be made more concrete:

- What is my purpose in being an adult educator?

- How would I describe my practice in relation to this purpose?

- How do I bring myself—my beliefs, values, assumptions, and preferences—into my teaching?

- How does my view of myself as a learner contribute to how I teach?

- How do I see the learners I work with?

- How do I determine the content of a course, workshop, or program?

- How do I allow for change and variation in my practice as I am practicing?

- What methods or strategies do I usually use and why?

- What is my view of evaluation of learning, and how is this translated into practice?

- What constraints or resistances influence my practice?

- How do I know when I have done well?

My response to some of these questions might look like this:

My purpose in being an adult educator is to facilitate individuals' learning and development, especially that which is empowering and transformative. In order to work toward this goal, I emphasize my relationship with students. I genuinely care for the people I work with, trust them, and respect them as people and as experienced professionals. I share my expertise, support learners, and challenge them to question what they already know and what they are learning.

I am conscious of my own learning and teaching style and my values and preferences, and I try, as much as possible, to bring who I am into the relationship with students. I do not hesitate to tell anecdotes about myself and my experiences, to share my mistakes and failures, and to wonder aloud about issues that I am struggling with.

I determine the content in most of my practice (except one-day or two-day workshops in collaboration with the participants). I may introduce the area or provide an overview if it is one that is unfamiliar to participants, and I may provide guidance as to some of the things that can be included, but in general, it is the participants who choose the specific topics to work with. This approach is derived from my assumption that the students I work with are experienced and knowledgeable professionals. The methods and strategies I use in my practice are those that foster support, challenge, and collaboration. That is, I use discussion, group work, team projects, and at times, individual or independent activities.

I believe that participants in my groups know better than I do what they have learned; therefore, I ask people to evaluate their own learning and, where grades are required by the institution, to assign a grade to represent that learning. I never challenge or change their evaluation. I choose not to exercise the power that is involved in the grading process.

I am fortunate in that I work primarily in graduate programs in adult education. There are very few constraints in my practice other than the constraints of scheduled meeting times (which I do not have in my online teaching) and some requirements as to deadlines for submitting grades.

I evaluate my own success based on comments from learners, people's learning projects, the nature and quality of the group processes, and the content and nature of discussions among members of the group. I also judge my success by how I feel at the end of the evening, day, or semester.

There is no one format or style for creating a perspective on education or a philosophy of practice, but this model may provide some guidance. I also enjoy philosophies that incorporate more creative components—poetry, drawings, photographs, or other illustrations.

Individuation: Teacher as Self

In Chapter Three, I describe Jung's ([1921] 1971) concept of individuation as the way in which people differentiate themselves from the general, collective society. People come to see how they are both the same as and different from others, and this is a transformative process. Transformation is the emergence of the Self. (I use *Self* [as opposed to *self*] to indicate the whole of the psychological construct that represents the psyche both conscious and unconscious.)

Learning who we are as teachers—within the community of teachers and also as individuals—is a transformative journey. New educators are finding their place, learning the expectations of their profession and their institution. They are trying to fit in, and during that process, they adopt the persona of teacher, the role of teacher that society expects of them. With experience and making meaning of that experience, teachers find their own way that is sometimes different from and sometimes the same as the teacher persona. In our research on how educators become authentic (a transformative process), my colleague and I found a clear developmental pattern (Cranton and Carusetta, 2004b). An outline of that pattern for each of the five facets of authenticity is given here:

Self-Awareness

- Fragmentation of teacher-self and Self
- Struggling to understand Self as teacher
- Integration of Self into teaching
- Understanding of Self both separate from and the same as others

Developing Awareness of Others

- Concrete, specific, unquestioned perceptions
- Conscious of individual differences in relation to subject area acquisition
- Conscious of others' level of personal development
- Complex, multifaceted understanding of others' diversity

Developing Relationships

- One-dimensional relationship based on rules
- Articulation of preferred nature of relationship
- A variety of ways of relating to students in different contexts
- Relationship that emphasizes the development of others' authenticity

Developing Awareness of Context

- Inflexible rules and generalizations about context
- Awareness of the influences of context on teaching and authenticity
- Critical questioning of context issues
- Setting oneself apart from context—bucking the system if necessary

Developing Critical Reflection

- Critical reflection on specific skills
- Critical reflection on teaching, institutional norms
- Content and process reflection on broader issues
- Critical questioning of premises (Why is it important to . . .?)

At the beginning stages for each of the themes, the educator tends to follow the rules of the institution or organization, to categorize and see things in a more black-and-white fashion. As with most developmental models, people come to see the world in more complex ways, distinguish themselves from social expectations, and are able to hold seemingly contradictory points of view. Jung describes the analytic process as including awareness of personal unconscious contents such as dormant character traits, attitudes, and abilities followed by discovering your role as a social being—your place in the world where you fit according to your talents and abilities, your vocation. Then in the stage of transformation, you become more fully the person you were always meant to be. Conscious development replaces unconscious behavior; meaning replaces aimlessness (Sharp, 2001). The emergence of teacher as Self is the progressive advance of consciousness.

Through the kinds of activities and strategies described in this chapter, educators can consciously move through an individuation process that takes them into a clearer and better justified frame of reference for their practice and an ever-developing idea of who they are as teachers.

Summary

When I opened my book *Professional Development as Transformative Learning* (Cranton, 1996) with the sentence, "Educators are adult learners," a reviewer found this to be a trite statement, but I still wonder whether we think enough about the importance of our own learning and especially our transformative learning as practitioners. Through learning and development, we move away from a mechanistic kind of approach to selecting teaching techniques, we question our practice rather than repeating what we have done in previous sessions, and we become models for our learners.

Educators' awareness of themselves as people and practitioners is the foundation of transformative learning about teaching. I suggest a series of questions we can ask of ourselves in each of the psychological, sociolinguistic, and epistemic frames of reference.

Articulating our assumptions about teaching can be helped by structured activities such as criteria analysis and crisis-decision simulations, or through engagement in more intuitive, arts-based strategies. Any of the processes we use to help learners become aware of their assumptions—keeping a journal, writing a life history, doing critical incidents—can be turned into a way of understanding what assumptions we might be making in our work.

Engaging in critical self-reflection and questioning regarding our practice can be done within the framework of content, process, and premise reflection. What do we do? How did we come to do it that way? Why is it important? Participation in professional development activities, engaging in action research, and discovering the influence of social norms through film and fiction can also help us challenge our own thinking about teaching.

Dialogue is central to becoming a transformative learner about our practice. All too often, adult educators feel isolated and without support or challenge from others. I discuss a variety of strategies for setting up the circumstances that will foster good dialogue about teaching.

When we have a rationale or a vision for our work, we are able to make meaningful choices and to think about what we do in a way that is more likely to become transformative. In this chapter, I provide a set of questions that can be used to shape a guiding perspective on education.

Individuation is the process of distinguishing one's self from the collective of humanity and learning how we are both the same as and different from others. In the community of educators, individuation involves differentiating who we are as teachers from the teacher collective—the way teachers are expected to behave by the community, institution, and society in general. As one framework for viewing this developmental process, I present some results from my research on how people become authentic in their practice.

Palmer (2000) says it well:

> What a long time it can take to become the person one has always been! How often in the process we mask ourselves in faces that are not our own. How much dissolving and shaking of ego we must endure before we discover our deep identity—the true self within every human being that is the seed of authentic vocation. (p. 9)

References

Apps, J. *Teaching from the Heart*. Malabar, FL: Krieger, 1996.

Argyris, C., and Schon, D. A. *Theory in Practice: Increasing Professional Effectiveness*. San Francisco: Jossey-Bass, 1974.

Baumgartner, L. M. "An Update on Transformational Learning." In S. Merriam (ed.), *The New Update on Adult Learning Theory*. New Directions for Adult and Continuing Education, no. 89. San Francisco: Jossey-Bass, 2001.

Belenky, M. F., Bond, L. A., and Weinstock, J. S. *A Tradition That Has No Name*. New York: Basic Books, 1997.

Belenky, M. F., Clinchy, B. M., Goldberger, N. R., and Tarule, J. M. *Women's Ways of Knowing: The Development of Self, Voice, and Mind*. New York: Basic Books, 1986.

Belenky, M., and Stanton, A. "Inequality, Development, and Connected Knowing." In J. Mezirow, and Associates (eds.), *Learning as Transformation: Critical Perspectives on a Theory in Progress*. San Francisco: Jossey-Bass, 2000.

Berger, J. G. "Dancing on the Threshold of Meaning: Recognizing and Understanding the Growing Edge." *Journal of Transformative Education*, 2004, *2*(4), 336–351.

Boyd, R. D. "Trust in Groups: The Great Mother and Transformative Education." In L. S. Walker (ed.), *Proceedings of the Annual Midwest Research-to-Practice Conference in Adult and Continuing Education*. Ann Arbor: University of Michigan, 1985.

Boyd, R. D. "Facilitating Personal Transformation in Small Groups." *Small Group Behavior*, 1989, *20*(4), 459–474.

Boyd, R. D. *Personal Transformation in Small Groups: A Jungian Perspective*. London: Routledge, 1991.

Boyd, R. D., and Myers, J. B. "Transformative Education." *International Journal of Lifelong Education*, 1988, *7*, 261–284.

Brookfield, S. *The Skillful Teacher.* San Francisco: Jossey-Bass, 1990.

Brookfield, S. *Developing Critical Thinkers: Challenging Adults to Explore Alternate Ways of Thinking and Acting.* San Francisco: Jossey-Bass, 1991.

Brookfield, S. *Becoming a Critically Reflective Teacher.* San Francisco: Jossey-Bass, 1995.

Brookfield, S. "Transformative Learning as Ideology Critique." In J. Mezirow, and Associates (eds.), *Learning as Transformation: Critical Perspectives on a Theory in Progress.* San Francisco: Jossey-Bass, 2000.

Brookfield, S. "Unmasking Power: Foucault and Adult Learning." *Canadian Journal for the Study of Adult Education*, 2001, *15*(1), 1–23.

Brookfield, S. "The Praxis of Transformative Education: African American Feminist Conceptualizations." *Journal of Transformative Education*, 2003, *1*(3), 212–226.

Brookfield, S. *The Power of Critical Theory: Liberating Adult Learning and Teaching.* San Francisco: Jossey-Bass, 2005.

Brookfield, S., and Preskill, S. *Discussion as a Way of Teaching: Tools and Techniques for Democratic Classrooms.* San Francisco: Jossey-Bass, 1999.

Brookfield, S., Sheared, V., Johnson-Bailey, J., and Colin, S. "Racializing the Discourse of Adult Education." In R. J. Hill and R. Keiley (eds.), *The 46th Annual Adult Education Research Conference.* Athens: The University of Georgia, 2005, 337–344.

Buber, M. *Between Man and Man.* Glasgow: Fontana Library, 1961.

Campbell, V. N. "Self-Direction and Programmed Instruction for Five Different Types of Learning Objectives." *Psychology in the Schools*, 1964, *1*, 348–359.

Candy, P. *Self-Direction for Lifelong Learning.* San Francisco: Jossey-Bass, 1991.

Carter, T. *The Voice of Relationship: Transformative Learning Through Developmental Relationships in the Lives of Mid-Career Women.* Unpublished doctoral dissertation, George Washington University, 2000.

Clark, J. E. *Scholarly Writing: A Personal Odyssey.* Unpublished doctoral dissertation, Ontario Institute for Studies in Education, 2005.

Clark, M. C., and Wilson, A. L. "Context and Rationality in Mezirow's Theory of Transformational Learning." *Adult Education Quarterly*, 1991, *41*(2), 75–91.

Coady, M. M. *Masters of Their Own Destiny.* New York: Harper and Brothers, 1939.

Cohen, J. B. "Hatha-Yoga and Transformative Learning—The Possibility of a Union?" Paper presented at the Fifth International Conference on Transformative Learning, Teachers College, Columbia University, 2003.

Cohen, J. B. "Late for School: Stories of Transformation in an Adult Education Program." *Journal of Transformative Education*, 2004, *2*(2), 242–252.

Cohen, L. R. "I Ain't So Smart, and You Ain't So Dumb: Personal Reassessment in Transformative Learning." In P. Cranton (ed.), *Transformative Learning in Action: Insights from Practice*. New Directions for Adult and Continuing Education, no. 74. San Francisco: Jossey-Bass, 1997.

Collard, S., and Law, M. "The Limits of Perspective Transformation: A Critique of Mezirow's Theory." *Adult Education Quarterly*, 1989, *39*, 99–107.

Cranton, P. *Understanding and Promoting Transformative Learning*. San Francisco: Jossey-Bass, 1994.

Cranton, P. *Professional Development as Transformative Learning*. San Francisco: Jossey-Bass, 1996.

Cranton, P. "Individual Differences in Transformative Learning." In J. Mezirow, and Associates (eds.), *Learning as Transformation: Critical Perspectives on a Theory in Progress*. San Francisco: Jossey-Bass, 2000a.

Cranton, P. *Planning Instruction for Adult Learners* (2nd ed.). Toronto: Wall and Emerson, 2000b.

Cranton, P. *Becoming an Authentic Teacher in Higher Education*. Malabar, FL: Kreiger Press, 2001.

Cranton, P. *Finding Our Way: A Guide for Adult Educators*. Toronto: Wall and Emerson, 2003.

Cranton, P. "Authenticity." In L. English (ed.), *Encyclopedia of Adult Education*. London: Palgrave Macmillan, 2005a.

Cranton, P. "Not Making or Shaping: Finding Authenticity in Faculty Development." In S. Blossey (ed.), *To Improve the Academy*, vol. 24. Bolton, MA: Anker Publishing, 2005b.

Cranton, P., and Carusetta, E. "Perspectives on Authenticity in Teaching." *Adult Education Quarterly*, 2004a, *55*(1), 5–22.

Cranton, P., and Carusetta, E. "Developing Authenticity as a Transformative Process." *Journal of Transformative Education*, 2004b, *2*(4), 276–293.

Cranton, P., and Dirkx, J. "Integrating Theoretical Perspectives Through Online Dialogue." Paper presented at the 6th International Transformative Learning Conference, East Lansing, Michigan, 2005.

Cranton, P., and Knoop, R. "Assessing Psychological Type: The PET Type Check." *General, Social, and Genetic Psychological Monographs*, 1995, *121*(2), 247–274. Also available at www.learningstyles.ca.

Cranton, P., and Roy, M. "When the Bottom Falls out of the Bucket: Toward a Holistic Perspective on Transformative Learning." *Journal of Transformative Education*, 2003, *1*(2), 86–98.

Cunningham, P. "From Freire to Feminism: The North American Experience with Critical Pedagogy." *Adult Education Quarterly,* 1992, *42*(3), 180–191.

Daloz, L. "The Story of Gladys Who Refused to Grow: A Morality Tale for Mentors." *Lifelong Learning,* 1988, *2,* 4–7.

Daloz, L. *Mentor: Guiding the Journey of Adult Learners.* San Francisco: Jossey-Bass, 1999.

Daloz, L. "Transformative Learning for the Common Good." In J. Mezirow, and Associates (eds.), *Learning as Transformation: Critical Perspectives on a Theory in Progress.* San Francisco: Jossey-Bass, 2000.

Della-Dora, D., and Blanchard, L. J. (eds.), *Moving Toward Self-Directed Learning: Highlights of Relevant Research and of Promising Practices.* Alexandria, VA: Association for Supervision and Curriculum Development, 1979.

Dewey, J. *How We Think.* New York: Heath, 1933.

Dewey, J. *Experience and Education.* New York: Collier Books, 1938.

Dirkx, J. "Nurturing Soul in Adult Education." In P. Cranton (ed.), *Transformative Learning in Action: Insights from Practice.* New Directions for Adult and Continuing Education, no. 74. San Francisco: Jossey-Bass, 1997.

Dirkx, J. "Transformative Learning Theory in the Practice of Adult Education: An Overview." *PAACE Journal of Lifelong Learning,* 1998, *7,* 1–14.

Dirkx, J. "After the Burning Bush: Transformative Learning as Imaginative Engagement with Everyday Experience." In C. A. Wiessner, S. Meyer, and D. Fuller (eds.), *Challenges of Practice: Transformative Learning in Action.* Proceedings of the Third International Conference on Transformative Learning, Teachers College, Columbia University, 2000.

Dirkx, J. "Images, Transformative Learning and the Work of Soul." *Adult Learning,* 2001a, *12*(3), 15–16.

Dirkx, J. "The Power of Feelings: Emotion, Imagination, and the Construction of Meaning in Adult Learning." In S. Merriam (ed.), *The New Update on Adult Learning Theory.* New Directions for Adult and Continuing Education, no. 89. San Francisco: Jossey-Bass, 2001b.

Dominicé, P. *Learning from Our Lives: Using Educational Biographies with Adults.* San Francisco: Jossey-Bass, 2000.

Ebert, O., Burford, M. L., and Brian, D. "Highlander: Education for Change." *Journal of Transformative Education,* 2003, *1*(4), 321–340.

English, L. "Feminine/Feminist: A Poststructural Reading of Relational Learning in Women's Social Action Organizations. In D. Clover (ed.), *Proceedings of the Joint International Conference of the Adult Education Research Conference and the Canadian Association for Studies in Adult Education* (pp. 136–141). University of Victoria, British Columbia, May, 2004.

English, L., and Gillen, M. (eds.). *Addressing the Spiritual Dimensions of Adult Learning: What Educators Can Do.* New Directions for Adult and Continuing Education, no. 85. San Francisco: Jossey-Bass, 2000.

Feller, A., Jensen, A., Marie, D., Peddigrew, B., Clinchard-Sepeda, L., and Campbell, E. "Quadrinity Online: Toward a Fuller Expression of Transformative Learning." *Journal of Transformative Education*, 2004, *2*(3), 219–230.

Fenwick, T. "Questioning the Concept of the Learning Organization." In S. M. Scott, B. Spencer, and A. M. Thomas (eds.), *Learning for Life: Canadian Readings in Adult Education.* Toronto: Thompson, 1998.

Fenwick, T. "Expanding Conceptions of Experiential Learning: A Review of the Five Contemporary Perspectives on Cognition." *Adult Education Quarterly*, 2000, *50*(4), 243–272.

Flanagan, J. "The Critical Incident Technique." *Psychological Bulletin*, 1954, *51*, 132–136.

Foucault, M. *Power/Knowledge: Selected Interviews and Other Writings, 1972–1977.* New York: Pantheon, 1980.

Frankl, V. *Man's Search for Meaning.* New York: Touchstone, 1984.

Freire, P. *Pedagogy of the Oppressed.* New York: Herder and Herder, 1970.

Gardner, H., Kornhaber, M. L., and Wake, W. K. *Intelligence: Multiple Perspectives.* New York: Harcourt Brace, 1996.

Gillen, M. "Spiritual Lessons from the Antigonish Movement." In S. M. Scott, B. Spencer, and A. M. Thomas (eds.), *Learning for Life: Canadian Readings in Adult Education.* Toronto: Thompson Educational Publishing, 1998.

Gilly, M. S. "Experiencing Transformative Education in the 'Corridors' of a Nontraditional Doctoral Program." *Journal of Transformative Education*, 2004, *2*(3), 231–242.

Goleman, D. *Working with Emotional Intelligence.* New York: Bantam Books, 1998.

Gozawa, J. "Transforming Learning as Disorienting Dilemma." In C. A. Wiessner, S. R. Meyer, N. Pfhal, and P. Neaman (eds.), *Transformative Learning in Action: Building Bridges Across Contexts and Disciplines.* Proceedings of the Fifth International Conference on Transformative Learning, Teachers College, Columbia University, 2003.

Greene, M. *Releasing the Imagination: Essays on Education, the Arts, and Social Change.* San Francisco: Jossey-Bass, 1995.

Griffin, V. "Holistic Learning." In T. Barer Stein and M. Kompf (eds.), *The Craft of Teaching Adults* (3rd ed.). Toronto: Culture Concepts, 2001.

Gunnlaugson, O. "Toward an Integral Education for the Ecozoic Era: A Case Study in Transforming the Glocal Learning Community of Holma

College of Integral Studies." *Journal of Transformative Education*, 2003, 2(4), 313–335.

Habermas, J. *Knowledge and Human Interests*. Boston: Beacon Press, 1971.

Habermas, J. *The Theory of Communicative Action*. Boston: Beacon Press, 1984.

Harrison, J. *Learning and Living 1790–1960*. London: Routledge and Kegan Paul, 1961.

Hart, M. "Critical Theory and Beyond: Further Perspectives on Emancipatory Education." *Adult Education Quarterly*, 1990, 40, 125–138.

Hayes, E., and Flannery, D. *Women as Learners: The Significance of Gender in Adult Learning*. San Francisco: Jossey-Bass, 2000.

Herman, L. "Engaging the Disturbing Images of Evil." In C. A. Wiessner, S. R. Meyer, N. Pfhal, and P. Neaman (eds.), *Transformative Learning in Action: Building Bridges Across Contexts and Disciplines*. Proceedings of the Fifth International Conference on Transformative Learning, Teachers College, Columbia University, 2003.

Hillman, J. "Peaks and Vales." In B. Sells (ed.), *Working with Images*. Woodstock, CT: Spring Publications, 2000.

Hollis, J. *Eden Project: In Search of the Magical Other*. Toronto: Inner City Books, 1998.

Hollis, J. *Creating a Life: Finding Your Individual Path*. Toronto: Inner City Books, 2001.

Jarvis, P. *Paradoxes of Learning: Becoming an Individual in Society*. San Francisco: Jossey-Bass, 1992.

Johnson, R. "Autobiography and Transformative Learning: Narrative in Search of Self." *Journal of Transformative Education*, 2003, 1(3), 227–245.

Jung, C. *Analytical Psychology: Its Theory and Practice*. New York: Random House, 1968.

Jung, C. *Psychological Types*. Princeton: Princeton University Press, 1971. (Originally published in 1921.)

Kasl, E., and Elias, D. "Creating New Habits of Mind in Small Groups." In J. Mezirow, and Associates (eds.), *Learning as Transformation: Critical Perspectives on a Theory in Progress*. San Francisco: Jossey-Bass, 2000.

Kasl, E., Marsick, V. J., and Dechant, K. "Teams as Learners: A Research-Based Model of Team Learning." *Journal of Applied Behavioral Science*, 1997, 33, 227–246.

Kegan, R. "What 'Form' Transforms? A Constructive-Developmental Approach to Transformative Learning." In J. Mezirow, and Associates (eds.), *Learning as Transformation: Critical Perspectives on a Theory in Progress*. San Francisco: Jossey-Bass, 2000.

King, P., and Kitchener, K. *Developing Reflective Judgment*. San Francisco: Jossey-Bass, 1994.

Knowles, M. *Self-Directed Learning: A Guide for Learners and Teachers*. Chicago: Follett, 1975.

Knowles, M. *The Modern Practice of Adult Education: From Pedagogy to Andragogy*. New York: Cambridge, 1980.

Kolb, D. *Experiential Learning: Experience as the Source of Learning and Development*. Upper Saddle River, NJ: Prentice Hall, 1984.

Kolb, D. *Learning Style Inventory*. Boston: Hay/McBer, 1999.

Kuhne, G. W., and Quigley, B. A. "Understanding and Using Action Research in Practice Settings." In B. A. Quigley and G. W. Kuhne (eds.), *Creating Practical Knowledge Through Action Research: Posing Problems, Solving Problems, and Improving Daily Practice*. New Directions for Adult and Continuing Education, no. 73. San Francisco: Jossey-Bass, 1997, 23–40.

Lange, E. "Transformative and Restorative Learning: A Vital Dialetic for Sustainable Societies." *Adult Education Quarterly*, 2004, *54*(2), 121–139.

Lennard, D., Thompson, T., and Booth, G. "The Artist's Inquiry: Fostering Transformative Learning Through the Arts." In C. A. Wiessner, S. R. Meyer, N. Pfhal, and P. Neaman (eds.), *Transformative Learning in Action: Building Bridges Across Contexts and Disciplines*. Proceedings of the Fifth International Conference on Transformative Learning, Teachers College, Columbia University, 2003.

Lin, L., and Cranton, P. "Dancing to Different Drummers: Individual Differences and Online Learning." *Creative College Teaching Journal*, 2004, *1*(1), 30–40.

Lindeman, E. C. *The Meaning of Adult Education*. New York: New Republic, 1926.

Livneh, C., and Livneh, H. "Continuing Professional Education Among Educators: Predictions of Participation in Learning Activities." *Adult Education Quarterly*, 1999, *49*(2), 91–106.

MacKeracher, D. *Making Sense of Adult Learning* (2nd ed.). Toronto: University of Toronto Press, 2004.

Marcuse, H. *The Aesthetic Dimension: Toward a Critique of Marxist Aesthetics*. Boston: Beacon Press, 1978.

Markos, L., and McWhinney, W. "Editors' Perspectives: Building On and Toward a Shared Vision." *Journal of Transformative Education*, 2004, *2*(2), 75–79.

Merriam, S. "The Role of Cognitive Development in Mezirow's Transformative Learning Theory." *Adult Education Quarterly*, 2004, *55*(1), 60–68.

Merriam, S., and Brockett, R. *The Profession and Practice of Adult Education: An Introduction*. San Francisco: Jossey-Bass, 1997.

Merriam, S., and Caffarella, R. *Learning in Adulthood: A Comprehensive Guide*. San Francisco: Jossey-Bass, 1999.

Mezirow, J. *Education for Perspective Transformation: Women's Reentry Programs in Community Colleges*. New York: Center for Adult Education, Teachers College, Columbia University, 1975.

Mezirow, J. "Perspective Transformation," *Adult Education*, 1978, *28*, 100–110.

Mezirow, J. "A Critical Theory of Adult Learning and Education." *Adult Education*, 1981, *32*, 3–24.

Mezirow, J. "Concept and Action in Adult Education." *Adult Education Quarterly*, 1985a, *35*, 142–151.

Mezirow, J. "A Critical Theory of Self-Directed Learning." In S. Brookfield (ed.), *Self-Directed Learning: From Theory to Practice*. New Directions for Continuing Education, no. 25. San Francisco: Jossey-Bass, 1985b.

Mezirow, J. "Transformative Learning and Social Action: A Response to Collard and Law." *Adult Education Quarterly*, 1989, *39*, 169–175.

Mezirow, J. *Transformative Dimensions of Adult Learning*. San Francisco: Jossey-Bass, 1991.

Mezirow, J. "Transformative Theory out of Context." *Adult Education Quarterly*, 1997, *48*(1), 60–62.

Mezirow, J. "Learning to Think Like an Adult." In J. Mezirow, and Associates (eds.), *Learning as Transformation: Critical Perspectives on a Theory in Progress*. San Francisco: Jossey-Bass, 2000.

Mezirow, J. "Transformative Learning as Discourse." *Journal of Transformative Education*, 2003a, *1*(1), 58–63.

Mezirow, J. "Epistemology of Transformative Learning." In C. Weissner, S. Meyer, N. Pfhal, and P. Ncaman (eds.), *Transformative Learning in Action: Building Bridges Across Contexts and Disciplines*. Proceedings of the Fifth International Conference on Transformative Learning, Teachers College, Columbia University, 2003b.

Mezirow, J. "Forum Comment on Sharan Merriam's 'The Role of Cognitive Development in Mezirow's Transformational Learning Theory.'" *Adult Education Quarterly*, 2004, *55*(1), 69–70.

Mezirow, J., and Associates. *Fostering Critical Reflection in Adulthood: A Guide to Transformative and Emancipatory Learning*. San Francisco: Jossey-Bass, 1990.

Mezirow, J., and Associates (eds.). *Learning as Transformation: Critical Perspectives on a Theory in Progress*. San Francisco: Jossey-Bass, 2000.

Moore, J. "Is Higher Education Ready for Transformative Learning? A Question Explored in the Study of Sustainability." *Journal of Transformative Education*, 2005, *3*(1), 76–91.

Moore, T. *The Re-enchantment of Everyday Life*. New York: HarperCollins, 1996.

Myers, I. B. *Gifts Differing* (7th ed.). Palo Alto, CA: Consulting Psychologists Press, 1985.

Nesbit, T. "Class and Teaching." In R. St. Clair, and J. A. Sandlin (eds.), *Promoting Critical Practice in Adult Education*. New Directions for Adult and Continuing Education, no. 102. San Francisco: Jossey-Bass, 2004.

Newman, M. *Defining the Enemy: Adult Education in Social Action*. Sydney, Australia: Victor Stewart, 1994.

O'Hara, M. "Cultivating Consciousness: Carl R. Rogers's Person-Centered Group Process as Transformative Andragogy." *Journal of Transformative Education*, 2003, *1*(1), 64–79.

O'Sullivan, E. "The Ecological Terrain of Transformative Learning: A Vision Statement." In C. A. Wiessner, S. R. Meyer, N. Pfhal, and P. Neaman (eds.), *Transformative Learning in Action: Building Bridges Across Contexts and Disciplines*. Proceedings of the Fifth International Conference on Transformative Learning, Teachers College, Columbia University, 2003.

Palmer, P. *The Courage to Teach: Exploring the Inner Landscape of a Teacher's Life*. San Francisco: Jossey-Bass, 1998.

Palmer, P. *Let Your Life Speak: Listening for the Voice of Vocation*. San Francisco: Jossey-Bass, 2000.

Palmer, P. *A Hidden Wholeness: The Journey Toward an Undivided Life*. San Francisco: Jossey-Bass, 2004.

Perry, W. G. *Forms of Intellectual and Ethical Development in the College Years*. Austin, TX: Holt, Rinehart, & Winston, 1970.

Progoff, I. *At a Journal Workshop: Writing to Access the Power of the Unconscious and Evoke Creative Ability*. New York: Penguin Putnam, 1992.

Quindlen, A. *Blessings*. New York: Random House, 2002.

Robinson, P. "Meditation: Its Role in Transformative Learning and the Fostering of an Integrative Vision for Higher Education." *Journal of Transformative Education*, 2004, *2*(2), 107–122.

Sawyer, L. "Transformative Learning at the Intersection of Body, Mind, and Spirit." In C. A. Wiessner, S. R. Meyer, N. Pfhal, and P. Neaman (eds.), *Transformative Learning in Action: Building Bridges Across Contexts and Disciplines*. Proceedings of the Fifth International Conference on Transformative Learning, Teachers College, Columbia University, 2003.

Scott, S. "The Grieving Soul in the Transformation Process." In P. Cranton (ed.), *Transformative Learning in Action: Insights from Practice*. New Directions for Adult and Continuing Education, no. 74. San Francisco: Jossey-Bass, 1997.

Scott, S. "The Social Construction of Transformation." *Journal of Transformative Education,* 2003, *1*(3), 264–284.

Selman, G. "The Enemies of Adult Education." *Canadian Journal of University Continuing Education,* 1989, *15,* 68–81.

Senge, P. M. *The Fifth Discipline: The Art and Practice of the Learning Organization.* New York: Doubleday, 1990.

Shahjahan, R. A. "Centering Spirituality in the Academy: Toward a Transformative Way of Teaching and Learning." *Journal of Transformative Education,* 2004, *2*(4), 294–312.

Sharp, D. *Digesting Jung: Food for the Journey.* Toronto: Inner City Books, 2001.

Smith, S. "Insider and Outsider Status: An African American Perspective." In M. Wise and M. Glowacki-Dudka (eds.), *Embracing and Enhancing the Margins of Adult Education.* New Directions for Adult and Continuing Education, no. 104. San Francisco: Jossey-Bass, 2004, 57–65.

Sokol, A., and Cranton, P. "Transforming, not Training." *Adult Learning,* 1998, *9*(3), 14–16.

Taylor, E. "Building upon the Theoretical Debate: A Critical Review of the Empirical Studies of Mezirow's Transformative Learning Theory." *Adult Education Quarterly,* 1997, *48,* 32–57.

Taylor, E. "Analyzing Research on Transformative Learning Theory." In J. Mezirow, and Associates (eds.), *Learning as Transformation: Critical Perspectives on a Theory in Progress.* San Francisco: Jossey-Bass, 2000a.

Taylor, E. "Fostering Transformative Learning in the Adult Education Classroom: A Review of the Empirical Studies." In C. A. Wiessner, S. Meyer, and D. Fuller (eds.), *Challenges of Practice: Transformative Learning in Action.* Proceedings of the Third International Conference on Transformative Learning, Teachers College, Columbia University, 2000b.

Taylor, K. "Teaching with Developmental Intention." In J. Mezirow, and Associates (eds.), *Learning as Transformation: Critical Perspectives on a Theory in Progress.* San Francisco: Jossey-Bass, 2000.

Taylor, K., Marienau, C., and Fiddler, M. *Developing Adult Learners: Strategies for Teachers and Trainers.* San Francisco: Jossey-Bass, 2000.

Tennant, M. "Perspective Transformation and Adult Development." *Adult Education Quarterly,* 1993, *44*(1), 34–42.

Tisdell, E. J. "Feminist Pedagogies." In E. Hayes and D. Flannery (eds.), *Women as Learners: The Significance of Gender in Adult Learning.* San Francisco: Jossey-Bass, 2000a.

Tisdell, E. J. "Spirituality and Emancipatory Adult Education in Women Adult Educators for Social Change." *Adult Education Quarterly,* 2000b, *50*(4), 308–335.

Tisdell, E. J. *Exploring Spirituality and Culture in Adult and Higher Education*. San Francisco: Jossey-Bass, 2003.

Tisdell, E. J., and Tolliver, D. E. "The Role of Spirituality in Culturally Relevant and Transformative Adult Education." *Adult Learning*, 2001, *12*(3), 13–14.

Torres, C. A. "Paulo Freire, Education and Transformative Social Justice Learning." In C. A. Wiessner, S. R. Meyer, N. Pfhal, and P. Neaman (eds.), *Transformative Learning in Action: Building Bridges Across Contexts and Disciplines*. Proceedings of the Fifth International Conference on Transformative Learning, Teachers College, Columbia University, 2003.

Transformative Learning Centre. *The Transformative Learning Centre*, Retrieved from http://www.oise.utoronto.ca/~tlcentre/index.htm, November, 2004.

Vella, J. *Learning to Listen, Learning to Teach: The Power of Dialogue in Educating Adults*. San Francisco: Jossey-Bass, 2002.

Vital Knowledge Software. PET Learning Styles Overview. Retrieved from www.learningstyles.ca, 2003.

Watkins, M. *Invisible Guests: The Development of Imaginal Dialogue*. Woodstock, CT: Spring Publications, 2000.

Watkins, K., and Marsick, V. J. *Sculpting the Learning Organization: Lessons in the Art and Science of Systemic Change*. San Francisco: Jossey-Bass, 1993.

Wiessner, C. A. "Passin' It On." In C. A. Wiessner, S. Meyer, and D. Fuller (eds.), *Challenges of Practice: Transformative Learning in Action*. Proceedings of the Third International Conference on Transformative Learning, Teachers College, Columbia University, 2000.

Wiessner, C. A. "Where Have We Been? Where Are We Going? A Critical Reflection on a Collaborative Inquiry." *SCUTREA 2005 Conference Proceedings*, University of Sheffield, UK, 2004.

Wiessner, C. A., Meyer, S. R., Pfhal, N., and Neuman, P. (eds.). *Transformative Learning in Action: Building Bridges Across Contexts and Disciplines*. Proceedings of the Fifth International Conference on Transformative Learning, Teachers College, Columbia University, 2003.

Wiessner, C. A., and Mezirow, J. "Theory Building and the Search for Common Ground." In J. Mezirow, and Associates (eds.), *Learning as Transformation: Critical Perspectives on a Theory in Progress*. San Francisco: Jossey-Bass, 2000.

Yorks, L., and Marsick, V. J. "Organizational Learning and Transformation." In J. Mezirow, and Associates (eds.), *Learning as Transformation: Critical Perspectives on a Theory in Progress*. San Francisco: Jossey-Bass, 2000.

Yukl, G. *Leadership in Organizations* (2nd ed.). Upper Saddle River, NJ: Prentice-Hall, 1989.

Index